D1565933

FDR's Body Politics

NUMBER EIGHT
Presidential Rhetoric Series
Martin J. Medhurst
General Editor

FDR's Body Politics
The Rhetoric of Disability

Davis W. Houck and Amos Kiewe

Texas A&M University Press

COLLEGE STATION

Photos courtesy Franklin D. Roosevelt Presidential Library.

Davis W. Houck, "Reading the Body in the Text: FDR's 1932 Speech to the Democratic National Convention," *The Southern Communication Journal* 63 (1997), 20–36, and Amos Kiewe, "A Dress Rehearsal for a Presidential Campaign: FDR's Embodied 'Run' for the 1928 New York Governorship," *The Southern Communication Journal* 64 (1999), 155–67, are reprinted with the permission of the Southern States Communication Association.

Amos Kiewe, "The Body as Proof: Franklin D. Roosevelt's Preparations for the 1932 Presidential Race," *Argumentation & Advocacy* 36 (1999), 88–100, is reprinted with the permission of the American Forensics Association.

Library of Congress Cataloging-in-Publication Data

Houck, Davis W.

FDR's body politics : the rhetoric of disability /
Davis W. Houck and Amos Kiewe.—1st ed.

p. cm.—(Presidential rhetoric series ; no. 8)

Includes bibliographical references and index.

ISBN 1-58544-233-X (cloth : alk. paper)

1. Roosevelt, Franklin D. (Franklin Delano), 1882-1945—Health. 2. Roosevelt, Franklin D. (Franklin Delano), 1882-1945—Language . 3. Roosevelt, Franklin D. (Franklin Delano), 1882-1945—Public opinion. 4. Physical fitness—Political aspects—United States—History—20th century. 5. Rhetoric—Political aspects—United States—History—20th century. 6. Body, Human—Social aspects—United States—History—20th century. 7. People with disabilities—United States—Biography. 8. Presidents—United States—Biography. 9. United States—Politics and government—1933-1945. 10. Public opinion—United States.

I. Kiewe, Amos. II. Title. III. Series.

E807 .H725 2003

973.917'092—dc21

2002012925

CONTENTS

ILLUSTRATIONS

PREFACE

THE TITLE OF OUR BOOK is taken from a speech that Franklin D. Roosevelt gave on November 7, 1932—the last night of his life that he was not president-elect or president. The speech was delivered to friends, neighbors, and well-wishers near his life-long home in Hyde Park, New York. Clearly contemplating his own victory, the candidate reflected, "Favor comes because for a brief moment in the great space of human change and progress some general human purpose finds in him a satisfactory embodiment." It was a fitting statement for a man who for eleven years worked relentlessly to rendezvous with that "brief moment." Our book chronicles that work—work we take to be fundamentally rhetorical.

Rhetoric and FDR are usually coupled within the context of his famous "fireside chats," or his uplifting First Inaugural Address, or his resolute War Message. Our approach to rhetoric is a bit different, perhaps a bit more expansive. With our colleagues across the humanities, we recognize the fundamental role of the human body in transactions of influence. To put it somewhat punningly, bodies matter. Presidential bodies matter most of all. To become president, FDR knew that in public he had to appear to be healthy—someone who could appear to walk, who looked healthy, and who interacted with others. This meant that FDR's body politics needed to be transacted very publicly, very often, and before large crowds. But when he was not out among the people showcasing his health, FDR had a number of people doing surrogate body work for him—textually, but body work all the same. Thus our study moves across texts that feature words, texts that feature FDR's physical presence, and some that highlight both—but all with an eye toward one thing: influence. Never should we lose sight of the fact that FDR's mission was singular: to become president. And he knew that crippled bodies were not "fit" for that job, less "fit" than they are today, it seems. As such, we try to keep our eye squarely on how FDR's body rhetorics played with his myriad audiences.

Over the several years during which our odyssey with FDR has taken shape, we have incurred many debts. Both Florida State University and

Syracuse University have been very generous in granting us leave time as well as financial support to complete this project. Several colleagues and friends have been most generous with their editorial talents, notably Kay Picart from Florida State, Marty Medhurst at Texas A&M University, and Vanessa Beasley, also from Texas A&M University. We also owe a special thank you to Geoffrey C. Ward, whose book, *A First-Class Temperament,* remains a first-class treatment of FDR and his struggles with infantile paralysis. Not only has Geoff paved the way for many FDR scholars, but he has also been very generous in lending to our project, at every stage, his ear and his encouragement.

One of the great frustrations in making the case for the primacy of disability in FDR's electoral life involves source material. Specifically, primary source material related directly to FDR and polio is just plain hard to find. We think that FDR wanted it that way. Fortunately for us, we worked with some helpful and resourceful archivists. In particular, Mark Renovitch at the Franklin D. Roosevelt Presidential Library in Hyde Park has been a terrific help. The staffs at the Herbert Hoover Presidential Library in West Branch, Iowa, and the Hoover Institution on War, Revolution and Peace at Stanford University have also been helpful in our oftentimes "needle-in-a-haystack" searchings.

This book is our third together. And, as with all good "marriages," we have figured out what works through trial and error. We have each authored separate chapters, while editing, revising, and adding to the other's work. In that sense, our work is truly a partnership. The first author drafted chapters 1, 2, 6, 7, and 8. The second author drafted chapters 3, 4, and 5. As such, "firsts" and "seconds" are really a misnomer, symptomatic of alphabetical order rather than expenditure of effort. Our readers, we trust, will recognize that sensibility in the pages that follow.

Finally, thanks to our copy editor, Maureen Creamer Bemko, and the staff at Texas A&M University Press for taking an interest in this project—and for improving it.

FDR's Body Politics

1   Introduction

AT WEST POTOMAC PARK IN THE NATION'S CAPITAL on the morning of May 2, 1997, the forty-second president of the United States publicly dedicated a memorial to its thirty-second president. It was a memorial more than four decades in the making. Perhaps not surprisingly, controversy attended the unveiling of the $48-million, 7.5-acre memorial to Franklin D. Roosevelt. No stranger to controversy himself, Bill Clinton addressed that controversy directly in his brief remarks: "It was that faith in his own extraordinary potential that enabled him to guide his country from a wheelchair. And from that wheelchair," the president continued, "and a few halting steps, leaning on his son's arms or those of trusted aides, he lifted a great people back to their feet and set America to march again toward its destiny."[1]

But there was no wheelchair at the memorial in the spring of 1997.

Ten days earlier, on April 23, the president had previewed his "wheelchair" remarks. After intensive lobbying from the National Organization on Disability, Clinton suddenly changed his tack; he announced that he would immediately send legislation to Congress to modify the memorial. Franklin Roosevelt should be depicted not as the public knew him and saw him during his remarkable twelve years in office; rather, he should be remembered as his intimates knew him: as someone whose locomotion was frequently facilitated by a wheelchair. The deception should "officially" end.

The new and improved memorial, though, was rationalized by the president less on the grounds of historical realism and more on American exceptionalism: "By showing President Roosevelt as he was we show the world that we have faith that in America you are measured for what you are and what you have achieved, not for what you have lost."[2] And yet the contradiction in metaphysics was palpable; who Roosevelt was and what he had achieved could never be uncoupled from the body he had lost during the summer of 1921. By stipulating that Roosevelt be memorialized, in part, in a wheelchair, was the federal government not insisting on showcasing that loss, rendering it public and permanent in the nation's collective memory?

Bill Clinton was also on hand three and a half years later when the memorial was rededicated on January 10, 2001. Again he spoke. At the close of his presidency, Clinton again attempted to rhetorically transcend the specifics of Roosevelt's crippled body: "What matters most in life is the spirit and the journey of the spirit. And we lug along that journey whatever body God gives us and whatever happens to it along the way, and whatever mind we were born with."[3] To close the thought, Clinton might very well have written his own presidential epitaph: "But a clever mind and a beautiful body can themselves be disabilities on the spirit journey."

Nearly eighty years after infantile paralysis had invaded Franklin Roosevelt's body, the circle seemed finally to have closed on his disability. The deception was over. The story had finally been told. We would not disagree; the official story does seem to have reached closure—even if prolonged.

But we have another story to tell here. In part it is a very private story, played out in letters, diaries, and conversations far removed from the public spaces of presidential politics. At another level, though, our story is an exceedingly public one, for part of Roosevelt's rhetorical genius lay precisely in sustained disclosure. It is a story first and foremost about one man's unquenchable political ambition—but an ambition everywhere informed by a disabled body. It is also a story about how disabilities disable, how a culture transforms a bodily wound into a public stigma.

It is thus a story about rhetoric and about history and their interaction. To put the matter rather baldly: How does a crippled man become president in the context of a culture that elects only healthy bodies?

Deception, yes. But pitiless publicity, too.

The relationship between rhetoric and disability, of course, did not begin with Franklin Roosevelt; it has been with us from the beginning. We have only to consult Book II of *The Iliad* to witness the purportedly blind Homer making the connection. In an assembly of all the Achaeans—both kings and common soldiers—one man railed on against King Agamemnon and the nine-year siege at Troy. Homer the dramatist takes great care to describe not just the rhetorical "rantings" of Thersites but also, more importantly, his bodily appearance.

> Here was the ugliest man who ever came to Troy.
> Bandy-legged he was, with one foot clubbed,
> Both shoulders humped together, curving over
> His caved-in chest, and bobbing above them
> His skull warped to a point,
> Sprouting clumps of scraggly, woolly hair.[4]

Before uttering even a word to the gathered assembly, Homer has effectively disabled Thersites and his speech of dissent. Thersites' rhetoric is thus not inseparable from the speaking subject—in all his grotesqueness of physical appearance. In an age of primary orality in which nearly all rhetoric was embodied, this disfigured body presages his narrative demise.

But despite his lack of rank and despite his physical impairments, Thersites does not shy from poking fun at mighty Agamemnon's own body: "Still moaning and groaning mighty Atrides—why now? / What are you panting after now?"[5] Was Agamemnon's acquisitiveness the cause of his out-of-breath, beleaguered body? Thersites' body had presumably been disabled by nature (and then defined accordingly), whereas Agamemnon's selfishness for Trojan plunder was a disability engendered from within.

But Thersites was rhetorically disabling not only Agamemnon; he reserved perhaps his strongest disabling invective for his fellow soldiers: "How shameful for you, the high and mighty commanders, / to lead the sons of Achaea into bloody slaughter! / Sons? No my soft friends, wretched excuses / —women, not men of Achaea!"[6] Thersites had effectively feminized his audience through what is now a common twenty-first-century trope of soft bodies (feminine) and hard bodies (masculine). The irony to the assembled warriors and kings must have been palpable: A badly disfigured cripple was re-figuring his audience as the "truly" or "genuinely" disabled.

By hyperbolizing bodies in this segment of his epic, Homer's symbolic, corporeal punishment of Thersites is most predictable: "And he [Odysseus] cracked the scepter across his back and shoulders. / The rascal doubled over, tears streaking his face / and a bloody welt bulged up between his blades."[7] So much for freedom of expression in wartime. And so much for being kind to cripples. The symbolism of the scepter is a most arresting image here, standing metonymically for kingly authority, a king whose authority also authorizes speech. Thersites' beating is thus both symbolic and corporeal; his silence is administered at the hands of kingly Odysseus. And, of course, the very public nature of Thersites' beating and subsequent humiliation served as potent proof to any other potentially acrimonious Achaeans. Speech would be carefully policed by Odysseus, and that policing assumed a form most appropriate to warfare, that of bodily harm.

Homer's depiction of Thersites (and Odysseus) is instructive for our study of the twentieth century's most important president, Franklin Delano Roosevelt, in several ways. First, and most obvious, both men were physically impaired. But while Thersites could not hide his lameness, Roosevelt could and did—both verbally and visually. That both men's physical impairments were viewed culturally as disabling speaks to an important condition: Cultures invest bodily conditions with meaning and in so doing can valorize or admonish appropriately. Disability is not written in the stars—or on the body; rather, disability is a construction, defined and negotiated by a culture at a given point in time.[8] It means different things to different people at different historical moments. To say this is not to deny

the material fact of physical impairment; it is to affirm the fact that a physical impairment's meaning is never fixed or given. Like most meanings, it
is fluid, and this condition invites the researcher to interpret the manifold
meanings of disability within a given time and culture and to show how
such meanings have very material consequences for those labeled "disabled."

Second, bodies are terribly important rhetorical resources in an oral culture, and while Thersites' disabilities worked against him in such a cultural
milieu, Roosevelt tapped the resources of orality to his rhetorical advantage. While the aim of their work does not directly address the intersections
of rhetoric and disability, Roderick Hart, Lloyd Bitzer, Karlyn Kohrs Campbell and Kathleen Hall Jamieson, Carole Blair, Michel Foucault, and Kenneth Burke each emphasize that language is fundamentally an action, a
verb, something that does material work in the world.[9] And when that language is embodied orally by a speaker to an audience, that action takes on
additional layers of meaning. As Carroll C. Arnold notes in a very sugges-
tive essay, oral rhetoric, or rhetoric that is physically spoken by a speaker,
contains unique meanings different from those, for example, of a written
text.[10] Rhetoric that is oral is always "rhetoric-in-stress." Nearly thirty years
before the "arrival" of body criticism in rhetorical studies, Arnold asked a
terribly germane question: "Will I be able to command myself, including
my thoughts, under the conditions of orality?" Part of that command, one
that the post-polio Roosevelt perhaps instinctively understood, was of the
human body. Roosevelt, as we will document, went to great lengths to
"command himself," and he thereby authorized himself to command and
lead others. Without that public command of his crippled body, without
overcoming the "dimensions of risk to the self" that orality creates, Roosevelt would never have been elected governor or president.[11] Roosevelt
opted at critical moments in his pursuit of both offices to address myriad
audiences face-to-face. Such embodied public, highly scripted moments
functioned to present Roosevelt as a healthy candidate, certainly in command physically, who could meet the demands of either office. We would
do well not to overlook the public-ness of Roosevelt's bodily performances.
As Anne Norton notes, "The capacity to make oneself visible, to be seen, is
a prerogative, and hence a sign of power."[12] That Roosevelt could speak in
public at all is, of course, an important manifestation of power. That point
was certainly not lost at Troy.

Third, Thersites' genius as a rhetorician is asserted precisely at the point
where he re-figures disability—away from his own physical body and onto
the metaphorical bodies of Agamemnon and the Achaeans. Franklin Roosevelt's rhetorical genius would partake of similar resources; despite warn-
ings and whisperings about his frail health and crippled body, Roosevelt

would re-figure his opponents' bodies (Hoover and other Republicans) as diseased, crippled, and sedentary bodies incapable of feeling. In so doing, he would also re-figure his own polio-ravaged body as the healthy and robust body most suitable for dealing with the nation's "depressed" and prostrate state.

One of the telling ways in which Thersites re-figured his Achaean auditors is by feminizing them, referring to them as "soft," "wretched," and even specifically as "women." Femininity is perhaps the ultimate disability in archaic Greek culture, especially in the context of warfare. It was also a monumental disability in American electoral politics in the 1920s and 1930s. Even today, politicians must battle the "wimp factor," a not-so-subtle questioning of their masculinity. As Michael Kimmel notes, "Political figures . . . have found it necessary both to proclaim their own manhood and to raise questions about their opponents' manhood."[13] That manhood seems to begin and end with the body and its performance of masculinity; moreover, as R. W. Connell argues, "The constitution of masculinity through bodily performance means that gender is vulnerable when the performance cannot be sustained—for instance, as a result of physical disability."[14] Following his affliction in the summer of 1921, Roosevelt was never publicly labeled as a "woman," but his masculinity was clearly imperiled if not altogether compromised because he could no longer independently control his own body. That Roosevelt and chief political confidant Louis McHenry Howe were aware of this peril is attested to by Theo Lippman, Jr.: "Roosevelt and especially Howe always feared that part of the public did want a leader who was as physically able-bodied and impressive as he was mentally astute . . . [there was] a conscious or unconscious yearning for a symbol of masculinity in the state house or White House."[15] Only fully masculine men could attain the nation's highest elected office; thus would Roosevelt have to re-make and re-figure his own body.

But in comparing the circumstances of Thersites and Roosevelt, some might object that we are missing the point; after all, while Thersites was beaten into submission and silence by the kingly Odysseus, Roosevelt was not. He did, however, have to submit to a higher authority—namely, the American people. In 1932, they had no interest in seeing a "kingly" leader in a crippled condition. The public, then and now, needed to believe that the emperor still had clothes. Roosevelt complied with their wishes. Perhaps ironically, that silence about disabled bodies has carried over into academic scholarship, where only recently has disability emerged as a legitimate area of inquiry. Perhaps even the brave Thersites could not have envisioned a silence nearing three millennia.[16]

The silences surrounding disability also mirror the silences surrounding lived experiences. In characterizing recent academic work in rhetoric, Jack

Selzer notes, "Words have been mattering more than the matter."[17] Rhetorical texts have often taken on a life of their own, far removed from the material world that produces and sustains them. Whether the "cause" is deconstruction, as Selzer avers; scholars' fixation on the symbolic model, as Carole Blair argues; or rhetoric's divorce from the rational and "truth" of philosophy, as Brenda Jo Brueggemann and James A. Fredal, and James C. Wilson and Cynthia Lewiecki-Wilson suggest, the result is largely the same. Bodies have often been forgotten, and the words these bodies spoke have been divorced from their corporeal, material context.[18] In this study, we will attempt to mend the separation of minds and bodies, texts and contexts, the material and the symbolic.

Re-figuration, masculinity and femininity, orality, the social construction of disability, and the material conditions of disability—these are our theoretical markers as we attempt to follow Franklin Roosevelt to the nation's highest political office. Our aim, at first blush, is a simple one: to determine how Roosevelt was "able" to become president in light of his crippled condition. The standard histories of the period would have us believe that the election of 1932 was not about Roosevelt's body; instead, it was about a failed Hoover administration and a willingness to adopt the New York governor's emphasis on "bold, persistent experimentation."[19] No doubt, many in the nation had clearly had their fill of the "enlightened engineer" and his seemingly taciturn, out-of-touch ways. What this view fails to take into account, though, is the complexity of the situation—specifically that the "whispering campaign" against Roosevelt had gained considerable force and, for many, veracity by the fall of 1932. And, such rumors put Roosevelt in a difficult rhetorical bind: How could he address his fitness for office without invoking his disability? By this time, he and his advisors had established that even to mention his disability was to risk invoking that most dis-abling emotion, pity.[20] Thus was Roosevelt's disability both a material and a textual problem.

We argue that Roosevelt's response in the summer and fall of 1932 must be read against the backdrop of 1928 and 1930; that is, in winning New York's gubernatorial elections, Roosevelt had to confront the same whispering, doubts, and innuendo that he would confront in 1932. And while some of his strategies and tactics would change, the seeds of his success in 1932 were sown in his pursuit of New York's statehouse. It was here that Roosevelt would master the requisite appearance and vocabulary to offer tangible proof that he was indeed capable of doing the job, without making his auditors squeamish or mawkish by detailing the "truth" or extent of his disability. As we will detail, Roosevelt's was a performative politics in the literal sense; body and mind would merge on the campaign trail.

While our aim is a historical one, and the stock-in-trade of the historian is primary sources and very proximate secondary ones, history is always inflected with theory. What we must remember is that Roosevelt, in seeking elected office, was first and foremost a rhetorician. As such, he had multiple audiences to influence—and we take influence to be very complicated and multilayered, especially influence-in-context. While texts can be intoxicating things, we are not deconstructionists out to revel in the play or deferral of meaning. Real people cast real votes for real candidates based on real rhetoric—with real consequences. Therefore, in attempting to make sense of the real, we will try to locate Roosevelt's audiences with respect to such pivotal issues as the public's perception of polio; perceptions about candidates' travel; the role of the press in protecting Roosevelt; the complex relationship binding disability, masculinity, and politics; and the linguistic context so instrumental to political rhetoric.

Regarding this last category, linguistic or discursive context, it should be emphasized that every culture shares a certain vernacular; in fact, such a vernacular is part and parcel of that culture. One of the arguments we offer involves the linguistic context of "depression." While the metaphor these days is largely "dead," the predominant lexical markers for talking about the economic events following the stock market crash of 1929 involved health and sickness. Such a consequence, as we will attempt to demonstrate, was not inconsequential, especially in 1932 as the "depression" neared its peak.

Of course we are not the first, nor will we be the last, to write about Franklin Roosevelt and disability. Hugh Gallagher, Robert T. Goldberg, Jean Gould, Frank Freidel, and Geoffrey C. Ward have all written eloquently and with distinction on the subject.[21] Our originality lies in our treatment of his disability. Instead of seeing infantile paralysis as something that he "overcame," we see it as something far more complex. Roosevelt never "overcame" his disability. Crippling physical disabilities are never "overcome"; they are lived with. Our treatment of his disability, unlike others, is not larded exclusively with the personal. Roosevelt was a lonely man who was tight-lipped about his disability, and we know very little about how his affliction affected his psyche. And while we have the first-hand accounts from his wife Eleanor and from other associates regarding how his disability may have affected his political leanings, we are unable to do detailed psychobiography. As with so many things personal regarding Franklin Roosevelt, we simply do not know.

To summarize our aims, then, we advance eight arguments:

1. Roosevelt's disability was carefully concealed not only from the media, and thus the public, but also from some members of his own family.

2. The reason for that concealment had nothing to do with polio per se but with how the public attributed meaning to that affliction.

3. In running for governor of New York, especially in 1928, as well as for president, Roosevelt emphasized a visual rhetoric that drew attention to his ostensibly healthy body. The manifestation of this rhetoric took two main forms: an ability to walk or give the appearance that he could walk and extensive travel by automobile, train, and airplane.

4. Along with this visual rhetoric, Roosevelt used the spoken word to portray his own health, while denigrating the health of his opponents. Following his successful campaign of 1928, this verbal rhetoric involved metaphors of a healthy or a sickly body.

5. The material condition of Roosevelt's body was much less consequential to his political life than the public's understanding of what his disability meant.

6. Herbert Hoover and his associates actively hoped for a Roosevelt candidacy in 1932 so that the nation could see firsthand just how frail Roosevelt was.

7. The linguistic context of the early 1930s assisted candidate Roosevelt in his rhetorical efforts to construct a bodily understanding of the Great Depression.

8. The rhetorical strategies that Roosevelt employed to combat the constant "whispering" about his health were effective in helping to get him elected in 1928, 1930, and 1932.

Regarding this last argument, we should emphasize from the outset that ours is a study in political persuasion—effects, in a word. The topic of effects in rhetorical studies, and specifically the evidence needed to adjudicate claims of effect, has recently come under much scrutiny—and deservedly so.[22] While we do not attempt to measure the effects of Roosevelt's rhetorical strategies on public opinion in a numerical way, we opt for the next best evidentiary things: personal letters addressed to Roosevelt and his advisors, diary entries, memoranda, oral histories, and the reaction to Roosevelt's bodily performances recorded by the nation's newspapers. What emerges is a picture of a highly successful eleven-year campaign with the single aim of winning elections. Roosevelt's success, of course, was not attributable solely to his ability to appear healthy; nonetheless, as we will illustrate, the myriad appearances were often very consequential in accomplishing the needed rhetorical goal. While we cannot prove the historical contrary-to-fact- conditional, it is clear to us that without the appearance of a healthy body, Roosevelt would not have been elected governor in 1928, nor would he have become the thirty-second president of the United States.

In order to substantiate the aforementioned claims, we will proceed in a chronological fashion, one which begins with the terribly consequential days of early August, 1921. As we detail in the next chapter, Louis Howe and Eleanor Roosevelt's carefully orchestrated camouflaging of Roosevelt's bout with infantile paralysis at Campobello Island set the tone for a twenty-four-year deception. That deception, however, appears to have had a predictably ambivalent beginning. Using the family's surviving correspondence, we will show that Eleanor and Franklin Roosevelt and Howe appear to have resisted the diagnosis favored by Fred Delano, Roosevelt's uncle. Once the diagnosis had been accepted, though, the family and Howe plunged energetically into a public optimism that was largely unwarranted given the extent of the damage done to Roosevelt's thirty-nine-year-old body.

In chapter 3 we move to the immediate postpolio period in which Roosevelt attempted to re-learn and re-master his own body. In addition to undertaking these daunting tasks, Roosevelt and Howe engaged in a strenuous letter-writing campaign to persuade those in the Democratic party that he would soon be back in the political fold. Roosevelt was true to his word with his very important appearance at the 1924 Democratic National Convention. At the convention, Roosevelt officially launched his political comeback with the now-famous "Happy Warrior" speech that placed New York governor Al Smith's name in nomination. Shortly after the convention, Roosevelt discovered the warm mineral waters of a tiny resort community in Georgia known as Warm Springs. It was there that he learned how to give the appearance of walking.

Following Roosevelt's political reemergence in the summer of 1924 and his continued convalescence at Warm Springs, we move in chapter 4 to the politically pivotal year of 1928, when Roosevelt officially reentered electoral politics by running for governor of New York. We attempt to illustrate Roosevelt's first "body" campaign, in which he had to dispel rumors about his fragile health that were inadvertently fomented by his own initial reluctance to accept Al Smith's entreaties to run for governor.

In chapter 5 we then turn to the curious relationship between Republican operative and journalist Earle Looker and the Roosevelts. More specifically, with Roosevelt's reelection landslide in 1930, he suddenly became a frontrunner for his party's presidential nomination in 1932. Looker fancied himself instrumental in positioning Roosevelt as a strong, fit candidate for president. Though Roosevelt always kept Looker at arm's length, we detail the correspondence between the two that eventually resulted in the July, 1931, publication of Looker's ostensibly objective article, "Is Franklin D. Roosevelt Physically Fit to Be President?" This article appeared in *Liberty Magazine,* a high-circulation weekly.

Roosevelt had planned something dramatic for his possible nomination at the 1932 Democratic National Convention. That plan, as we argue in chapter 6, involved a carefully orchestrated flight from Albany to Chicago to receive the party's nomination in person, thereby becoming the first candidate to do so. In addition, a careful reading of the famed "New Deal" speech reveals a cluster of body metaphors—metaphors that functioned rhetorically to cripple Herbert Hoover while simultaneously casting Roosevelt as the fit, physically vibrant leader of the nation.

After covering the dramatic events of July, 1932, in chapter 7 we move to an examination of Roosevelt's fall campaign for the Oval Office. Against the advice of party leaders, Roosevelt did not wage a front-porch campaign in which the nation's media periodically assembled at Hyde Park or Albany. Instead, taking his cue from his highly successful campaigns in New York, Roosevelt orchestrated two cross-country train trips during which he showed his body—always standing—to the nation's electorate. The trips, according to campaign architects Howe, Jim Farley, and Raymond Moley, were principally intended not to present policy but to placate fears about the candidate's physical infirmities. Not only did Roosevelt display his body often but the discourse of the trips was that of health and sickness. Roosevelt strategically borrowed from the media's lexical preference for talking about the "Great Depression," thus positioning himself as the doctor most appropriate for the convalescing, enervated patient.

We close the book with a brief look at the political legacy of Roosevelt's crippled body, a body that is still contested at the level of public memory. We also speculate on the extent to which disability today is much more disabling than it was during Roosevelt's years in elected office.

2 Keeping Secrets

FRANKLIN ROOSEVELT had an extremely busy day on Wednesday, August 10, 1921.[1] After arriving at the family's summer cottage on Campobello, a Canadian island just off the Maine coast, on Sunday, August 7, Franklin had been entertaining his boss, Van-Lear Black. It was on Black's 140-foot steam yacht, the *Sabalo,* that Roosevelt had arrived at the family's summer retreat. Ever the expert yachtsman, Franklin had taken over skippering duties aboard the *Sabalo* during a difficult stretch of fog. After a day of baiting hooks for Black and his companions, as well as a misstep that resulted in Roosevelt falling overboard into the frigid waters of the Bay of Fundy, Franklin said goodbye to Black at noon on the following day, the ninth. Now he was free to frolic with his ever-eager children. So with sons James and Elliott and wife Eleanor, Franklin piloted the small family sailboat, the *Vireo,* out across Friar Bay for a day of sailing. The sail proved adventurous, as the family noticed tendrils of smoke coming from a nearby island. Franklin maneuvered the *Vireo* close to the shoreline so that the family could disembark to fight the small forest fire. With boughs from pine trees, the family successfully put out the embers and then headed back across Cobschook Bay past Friar's Head to the family's wooden slip. Layered with soot, and hot from the sun and exertion, Franklin challenged James and Elliott, along with Louis Howe's son Hartley, to run with him to the family's favorite swimming hole, Lake Glen Severn, two miles away. Each of the four swam across the narrow lake, then ran across yards of sandy beach to the Bay of Fundy for another dip. Franklin's energy amazed the boys, as he challenged them to run with him all the way back to the cottage.

Upon returning home, and still in his wet swimsuit, Franklin perused the mail, which had been delivered while he was away. He did not feel well, and he informed his wife that his back ached and that he might have a touch of lumbago. "I suggested," recalled Eleanor, "that he go to bed, and I'd bring him his supper, and that was the beginning of his illness."[2] Recalling that fateful series of events on August 10, he would note that he felt "'too tired even to dress. I'd never felt quite that way before.'"[3] He headed upstairs to change and to get into bed. It would be the last time that he ever walked up a set of stairs. Thus began Franklin Roosevelt's twenty-four-year battle with infantile paralysis. But on that Wednesday, the diagnosis was more than two weeks away.

On Thursday, as Franklin complained of pain in his lower back and legs, and as his temperature hovered at 102 degrees, Eleanor sent a local man to Lubec, Maine, via motorboat to get Dr. E. H. Bennett, a country doctor who also tended to the Roosevelts' summer aches and pains. Bennett was initially perplexed by the symptoms, suggesting some sort of muscular impairment perhaps brought on by the chills Franklin had experienced earlier in the week. When massage brought no noticeable improvements by Saturday, August 13, Eleanor and Dr. Bennett decided to solicit the best medical opinion they could get quickly. Fortunately for Dr. Bennett and Eleanor, Louis Howe was at Campobello, vacationing with his family. The gnomish, chain-smoking newspaper journalist had worked by Roosevelt's side for nearly a decade, first at the statehouse in Albany, and later in Washington, D.C., during Franklin's tenure as assistant secretary of the navy in the Wilson administration. According to Eleanor, who would grow very close to Howe with the onset of her husband's illness, Howe knew that because of his own physical deficiencies he would never make it in politics. But he did have "an enormous interest in being a King Maker: in so to speak, having power, and if he could not have it, if he did not expect to have it himself—he wanted it through someone whom he was influencing."[4] Following the events during the summer of 1921, Howe would never again leave Roosevelt's side—much to the dismay of Roosevelt's mother, Sara.

Howe journeyed with Bennett back to the doctor's home in Lubec and immediately began canvassing local resorts by telephone for the best available diagnostician. They happened upon a famous Philadelphia surgeon, Dr. William Williams Keen, who was vacationing in Bar Harbor. Despite his advanced age of eighty-four, Dr. Keen agreed to travel to Campobello immediately. Shortly after his arrival at 7:30 that evening, he conducted a thorough examination. His diagnosis was that a blood clot from a bladder congestion had lodged in the lower spinal cord, thus temporarily inhibiting Franklin's ability to move his legs, though not preventing him from sensing pain or touch. Upon Dr. Keen's recommendation, Eleanor immediately wired New York for a masseuse. In the meantime, as she wrote to Franklin's half-brother "Rosy" (James Roosevelt Roosevelt), "Louis and I are rubbing him as well as we can." Dr. Keen cautioned that the next ten to fourteen days would be crucial but that there was room for optimism: "The doctor thinks absorption has already begun as he can move his toes on one foot a little more which is very encouraging."[5]

But beyond the purported blood clot and Franklin's increasingly acute symptoms, Howe and Eleanor were already, just four days into the illness, thinking about potential political fallout. She closed her letter of August 14 to Rosy thus: "I do not want particulars to get in the papers so I am writing the family that he is ill from the effects of a chill and I hope will soon be better."[6] Howe expressed such vague but hopeful sentiments in a letter a few days later to a Mr. Townsend: "Franklin has been quite ill for some days and while his temperature is now normal and the doctor thinks he has started up hill he is still very weak as he was much run down when he arrived."[7] Even the suspicious reader could not have suspected untoward health based on Howe's epistle. Thus had the material and textual battle for Franklin's body begun.

Privately, Eleanor was less sanguine about her husband's health. Much of her pessimism was probably attributable to the fact that Franklin's bowels and bladder had quit working by Monday, August 15. Since Dr. Bennett could not be present indefinitely, he showed Eleanor how to catheterize her husband as well as to give him enemas. That husband and wife had not been intimate for more than three years could not have emboldened Eleanor's nursing. In a letter to Rosy dated August 18, Eleanor reported that while Franklin's "mental attitude" had improved, "he has of course times of great discouragement." Part of that discouragement also stemmed from the elderly Dr. Keen's uncertainty over his initial diagnosis. Eleanor reported, "Dr. Keen wrote us a long letter saying that the longer he reflected the more he inclined to discard the clot and think the inflammation had caused a lesion in the spinal cord which might be a longer business than his first estimate." Enclosed with Dr. Keen's letter was a bill for six hundred dollars. The uncertainty and her husband's acute pain weighed heavily on Eleanor. From the very beginning of the illness she grasped the gendered implications of severe illness and how such implications might devastate her husband: "I dread the time when I have to tell Franklin and it wrings my heart for it is all so much more work to a man than to a woman."[8] A man without a functioning body simply was not a man.

Dr. Keen's uncertainty, perhaps coupled with his exorbitant bill, troubled Eleanor, Howe, and Dr. Bennett. Eleanor had already acted on Keen's first diagnosis, bringing in Edna Rockey, a masseuse who doubled as a nurse, on August 16. Now that decision looked premature. Eleanor and Howe, though, were extremely fortunate that they had also been corresponding about Franklin's illness with his uncle, Frederic Delano. It was through this correspondence that a correct diagnosis would finally emerge. A letter from Fred to Eleanor dated August 20 reveals that nearly ten days into the illness, infantile paralysis was suspected as the real culprit. After seeking medical counsel in Boston, home to the most renowned specialists in the country, Uncle Fred reported to Eleanor, "The great Dr. [Robert W.]

Lovett was away but through Z. Grant I called up the Peter Bent Brigham hospital and they recommended Dr. [Samuel A.] Levine as their best man on Infantile Paralysis." Fred continued, "I saw Levine at 2:15 and read him your letter and Howe's letter and your last telegram. He said at once, as did Dr. Parker in Washington, that it was unquestionably Infantile Paralysis." Uncle Fred's next words must have nearly crushed the inwardly insecure Eleanor: "He [Levine] said you should stop the manipulations and massage as unwise so early in the game. His argument is that the disease attacks the nervous system and you must give the patient rest to rebuild, etc." Eleanor and Howe, along with Edna Rockey, had unknowingly been assisting the crippling disease: "The practice as to massage has changed and the Dr. says it is bad to begin it too soon."[9]

Perhaps to assuage Eleanor's guilt and self-doubts, Fred closed his letter with an unsparing view of the eighty-four-year-old Keen: "Dr. Keen all doctors seem to know. He is a fine old chap, but he is a Surgeon and not a connoisseur on the malady. I think it would be very unwise to trust his diagnosis. . . . Pardon my being so insistent, but you and Mr. Howe ask for my best judgment and I give it to you. I need not explain why the blood clot theory is not accepted but the doctors I have consulted both stated that could not be and gave their reasons."[10]

It is unclear who was more devastated by the diagnosis, Howe or Eleanor (Franklin was not informed). Echoing the concern for FDR's career that Eleanor expressed in her letter to Rosy, Howe gave a succinct statement of the political implications of FDR's illness: "'I'm not going to mention the word paralysis unless I have to. If it's printed, we're sunk. Franklin's career is *kaput*, finished.'"[11] Always the newspaper journalist who understood the power of rhetoric to affect perceptions, Howe knew that if Franklin's career was indeed finished, his was too.

At this point, it is interesting to speculate on Howe's seemingly hyperbolic reaction—one that had little to do with the material condition of Franklin's body and everything to do with the textual condition of bodily paralysis generally, and infantile paralysis specifically. That is, regardless of infantile paralysis's devastating effects on a person's body, the disease had an equally debilitating effect on how people perceived that body.

In her insightful book on polio in the nineteenth and early twentieth centuries, Naomi Rogers illustrates how polio was associated with the poor, the slum-dwelling immigrant, and with the unhygienic—all of whom were seen as "guilty carriers."[12] Even though Roosevelt's background ran counter to common wisdom about polio, at least initially he could not "escape" the associations of the disease. To make matters worse, early studies by the noted pathologist Simon Flexner led the medical community to believe that polio was primarily a neurological disease. To be infected, therefore, was to be infected in body and mind. Moreover, even with the rise of germ theory, moral rectitude was still linked to one's physical health. Rogers notes that "germs, in lay thought, did not spread randomly; infection depended on the class, ethnicity, and personal habits of individuals."[13] Also lurking in Howe's insistence on silence was his recognition of the way persons with some visible bodily handicap were treated. According to Hugh Gallagher, "In the 1920s, to be handicapped in some visible way carried with it social opprobrium. The handicapped were kept at home, out of sight, in back bedrooms, by families who felt a mixture of embarrassment and shame about their presence."[14]

The other variable in the increasingly complex equation is that Roosevelt's career aspirations were in electoral politics, one of the most visible, public occupations of all. It was also a male occupation. And the body in the early twentieth century did not contain the man; it was the man. In addition, primarily because of structural economic changes, early-twentieth-century American men sought to exercise that masculinity by increasing control over their own bodies.[15] With infantile paralysis, Roosevelt surrendered this control and was subjected to the public's equating 'not masculine' with 'feminine.' And a politician seen as feminine was an unelectable politician.

It is understandable, therefore, that Louis Howe and Eleanor Roosevelt would hold out hope that Dr. Keen was right and that Dr. Levine, not having seen the patient, was wrong. A note of denial began to creep into Eleanor's correspondence with Rosy, just days after Uncle Fred's proxy diagnosis. She began with Dr. Keen's diagnosis: "The doctors agree that there is no doubt but that F[ranklin] is suffering from the after effects of a congestion of the lower part of the spinal cord," but she added, "It is too early yet to say positively if all this [was] cause[d] from his chill and exposure which brought to a focus an irritation that had existed some time, or from an attack of Infantile Paralysis." Eleanor still hoped for Dr. Keen's diagnosis: "On Uncle Fred's urgent advice, . . . I have asked Dr. Keen to try to get Dr. Lovett here for a consultation to determine if it is I. P. or not. Dr. Keen thinks not."[16] That Lovett was the country's leading authority on the disease seemed not to have swayed Eleanor's faith in Keen's diagnosis—either the first or the second one.

Why Eleanor had not by August 24 sent a telegram to solicit either Dr. Levine's or Dr. Lovett's services, as Fred Delano had urged in his letter of August 20, and why she insisted that Dr. Keen contact Dr. Lovett instead of doing it herself or with Louis Howe's able assistance raises some vexing and important questions. Was she afraid of consulting Dr. Lovett for fear of what Uncle Fred claimed was "unquestionable"? Was her delay in acting simply caused by a delay in receiving Uncle Fred's letter of August 20? Was

she acting on her husband's behalf? Or could it have been that she was acting on Louis Howe's behalf? There is also the possibility that Dr. Keen or
Dr. Bennett urged her not to consult the Boston specialists. Whatever the
scenario, Uncle Fred felt troubled enough that he actually telephoned Eleanor on August 24. According to Eleanor, "To reach the telephone in Campobello we had to walk all the way to the village, so I went to the village,
and found his uncle, Fred Delano, on the telephone saying he felt that Franklin should be examined by a specialist in polio. This was an entirely new
idea to me, but I said of course, and he said he was coming up and would
bring Dr. Lovett with him and so the next day [August 25] they arrived, and
on arrival Dr. Lovett examined my husband with very great care, [and] at
once pronounced it polio."[17]

Eleanor's oral history testimony on the subject of Lovett's visit, in com-
bination with the surviving letters, suggests that someone on Campobello
Island might not have welcomed "the great Doctor," as Fred had earlier referred to him. First, it is clear from Eleanor's account that for Fred to call the
family on the island was a most serious intervention. The nearest telephone
was two miles from the Roosevelt cottage, at the home of Mrs. Etta Mitchell,
the telegraph and telephone operator. Fred was clearly somewhat desperate
at this stage of Franklin's illness. Second, that Fred actually accompanied
Dr. Lovett to Campobello suggests even more desperation, given that his
letter of August 20 urged Eleanor merely to send for a doctor via telegram.
Third, recall that Fred had earlier been unsuccessful in getting Dr. Lovett
on the case and thus had counseled Eleanor to contact the next best man on
infantile paralysis, Dr. Levine. This action again suggests some desperation.
And fourth, note that Eleanor claims in the oral history that the consultation by an expert "was an entirely new idea to me." Clearly, this could not
have been a new idea had she received Uncle Fred's letter of August 20. Perhaps the final piece of evidence that suggests a reluctance by Eleanor or
Howe to diagnose Franklin with infantile paralysis at Campobello Island is
that twelve days had elapsed between Dr. Keen's initial blood clot theory
and Dr. Lovett's correct diagnosis. Such a time period, even by 1921 standards, is a long time for a family to endure uncertainty over what Eleanor
termed a "mysterious ailment." That Dr. Keen considered Uncle Fred's
proxy expert diagnosis to be incorrect and that Eleanor was inclined to believe the octogenarian surgeon suggests that those closest to Franklin, and
perhaps even Franklin himself, were reluctant to yield to an expert diagnosis so grim. Given Franklin's political ambitions, and given the tremendous
sense of ostracism and isolation experienced by the physically handicapped, who could blame him, her, or them?

Three days after Dr. Lovett's accurate diagnosis, August 28, Uncle Fred
felt compelled to write to Eleanor and reassure her that she had done the

right thing: "I am so glad you decided to have Dr. Lovett and bad though it is, it is better for all to know just what has happened and what must be guarded against."[18] Fred, of course, was right; that he still needed to convince his nephew's wife of this situation again suggests a degree of denial.

Fred was wrong, though, on another count. Clearly, it had not been "better for all to know" what had happened to Franklin. In the very same letter, Fred revealed to Eleanor that "your Aunt Annie knows nothing of Franklin except that he has been very ill and is recuperating." He added, "The secret has been pretty well kept considering all the telegraphing, etc."[19] If the Roosevelts and the Delanos were good at keeping Franklin's true condition a secret from proximate family members, it is no surprise that the nation was completely in the dark as to his health. Just a day before, on August 27, the *New York Times* reported in its back pages that while Roosevelt had been seriously ill, he was now improving.[20] Louis Howe was clearly spinning his rhetorical magic with the nation's "newspaper of record."

Eleanor, with the aid of Rosy and Uncle Fred, had also been engaged in a bit of obfuscation with a most important family member, Franklin's mother, Sara. From the outset of the illness, Eleanor thought frequently of her mother-in-law and how best to break the news to her. Whether she could not face the prospect of telling Sara that her beloved son was seriously ill or whether she felt it more appropriate for Sara's stepson James (Rosy) to break the news, the letters do not reveal. Nonetheless, now that Franklin and Eleanor would be at Campobello for some time, they could not meet Sara, as originally planned, upon her return from Europe. "Do you think you can meet Mama when she lands," Eleanor wrote to Rosy. "She has asked us to cable just before she sails and I have decided to say nothing. No letter can reach her now and it would simply mean worry all the way home and she will have enough once here but at least then she can do things." She hoped that Rosy or Uncle Fred could bear the bad news: "I will write her a letter of quarantine saying he is ill but leave explaining to you or if you can't meet her to Uncle Fred or whoever does meet her."[21] As many have documented, the relationship between Eleanor and Sara was frosty at best, and perhaps Eleanor could now envision a scenario whereby she would somehow be blamed for Franklin's illness. Thus the expression of self-doubt for which the young Eleanor was famous: "I hope you will think I am doing right and have done all I could."[22]

Uncle Fred and Rosy, along with Eleanor's Aunt Kassie, met the *Olympic* as it reached port on August 31. The following day at 1:30 in the afternoon, Sara Roosevelt arrived at the family's wooden slip. Eleanor was there to meet her. Clearly, based on Sara's letter to her brother Fred the following day, Eleanor had done her best to defuse the severity of the situation. So had Franklin, who had greeted her, "'Well I'm glad you are back Mummy and I got up this party for you!'"[23] She reported to her brother, "[Franklin] had shaved himself [sic] and seems very bright and keen. Below his waist he cannot move at all. His legs (that I have always been proud of) have to be moved often as they ache when long in one position." It was clearly the brave face, the attitude, that impressed Sara: "He and Eleanor decided at once to be cheerful and the atmosphere of the house is all happiness, so I have fallen in and follow their glorious example. . . . Dr. Bennett just came and said 'This boy is going to get all right.' They went in to his room and I hear them all laughing, Eleanor in the lead!"[24]

Eleanor's careful choreography, from the good cheer, the dockside greeting, Dr. Bennett's optimism, to even the act of shaving her husband (he was still much too weak to use his hands and arms) must have added to the enormous stress that she was still under. Despite her playful boasts to Dr. Keen—"The nurse and I divide the nights and really I am not getting tired. It would be so much harder if I could do nothing for him and while I may not look very strong, I am never ill and I always tell my husband that my side of the Roosevelt family has far more vitality than his"—there was still great uncertainty as to how badly the virus had damaged her husband's nervous system.[25] There was also the very real prospect that she had unwittingly damaged the legs that her mother-in-law had "always been proud of," based on Dr. Keen's recommendations. Then too there was the financial strain; in addition to his initial bill of six hundred dollars, Dr. Keen submitted a bill of one thousand dollars for his visit on August 25. On top of these stresses, there was the tremendous artifice of it all. Just the day before Sara's arrival at Campobello, Franklin hit his emotional nadir. Dr. Bennett was so alarmed by his patient's behavior that he wrote at once to Dr. Lovett: "'ATROPHY INCREASING POWER LESSENING CAUSING PATIENT MUCH ANXIETY ATTRIBUTED BY HIM TO DISCONTINUANCE OF MASSAGE CAN YOU RECOMMEND ANYTHING TO KEEP HIS COURAGE AND MAKE HIM FEEL THE BEST IS BEING DONE OR TELL HIM THOSE CHANGES ARE UNAVOIDABLE.'"[26]

While Eleanor did her best to choreograph family matters, Louis Howe continued the deception for the news media. After its initial report of August 27, the New York Times reported on August 29 that Roosevelt had merely caught a heavy cold and was threatened with pneumonia but that he was now recovering slowly.[27] On September 10, one month removed from the onset of the illness, the Times moved the story from the back pages to report the good news that the former vice-presidential candidate was showing gradual improvement from the threat of pneumonia.[28] In the meantime, Howe thought long and hard about the logistics of moving Franklin from Campobello Island to New York City, all the while keeping a low profile in the newspapers.

Despite his wife's upbeat reports to family members, Franklin must have been having grave doubts. Unable to move his legs, unable to control his bowels or bladder, unable to use his arms and hands, unable even to sit up in bed and still battling a persistent fever—it is little wonder that Franklin questioned whether the God that had always been so generous to him had now deserted him.[29] It was under these trying conditions that Franklin received a rather remarkable letter from his Uncle Fred. We reprint it in full because the "fatherly advice" that Fred offers was a harbinger of the public face that Franklin would put on his new body and his new condition.

My dear Franklin,
I spent a restless night last night and thought a good deal about you, wondering how I could be of some service and as a result of that cogitation, I came to the conclusion that I might give you some "Fatherly" advice. It won't do any harm and it may do some good! I do not remember the school books['] definition of philosophy, but since I passed 40, I have worked out ideas of my own on the subject. To my mind Philosophy means in substance, "making the best of the situation," or in other words taking things as they are, analyzing the facts, above all not fooling yourself, and by intelligent reasoning determining the right course to pursue. I never worry, I accept things as they are, I "look forward and not back." I realize that you are up against a hard problem, and hard cruel facts, and yet I feel the utmost confidence that you will emerge a better and a stronger man. It will give you time for reflection and that alone is worth a good deal! In your rushing and busy life you have not had that. Now as to your recovery, the doctors and misses can do much. Experience can warn you what to avoid, but, after all, the constructive work of getting well depends largely on your own character, for though I have never been carried away with the preachments of the faith healers and the Christian Scientists, I think they have a kernel of truth in their dictum, a truth as old as time, and in the words of Molieri, "Je prends (if prad) mes bien ou je les troure." [I take my things where I find them.] Of course, you mustn't rush things, because the Doctors tell me it is unwise to do active work for several weeks, but when you do begin your attitude to yourself and to this recovery will mean everything. Marvellous cures have been effected by men I know, in consumption, paralysis, etc, by the will and determination of the patient, and I feel so confident of your background of health and good habits and of your courage and good temper, that I refuse to be cast down. This does not mean

that I am lacking in sympathy; that you have on every side and if prayers can save you, you do not have to lift your hand. My philosophy does not at all exclude the supernatural power of our Heavenly Father, but I do think there is more truth than poetry in the saying "God helps those who help themselves"! You know that I have paid considerable attention to physical training. It began with my desire to enter the Army. I drilled with a small squad during the summer of 1917 and later took up the Walter Camp work and have kept it up ever since. Indeed, I should not have passed a dozen Doctors if I had not gotten in pretty fit condition! I have, however, gained so much physically and in every other way from the experience that I have become an exponent of the work, and incidentally have learned from others and the books of some experts. Among these, I have come upon a book on "breathing"—(Vitallie breathing it is called) which I have found very helpful and when you get back home and settled down to "hard work," I will send it to you for it is just the thing to do in bed when none of the family is about. Well, dear boy, this preachment is perhaps enough for to day! I promise not to repeat on this subject. I saw quite a little of Mr. Howe in N.Y. and he told us all about you in a most satisfactory way. He will be a most valuable aide and I am glad you have him by you. Furthermore, the arrangement you have made with Mr. Black and Mr. Hamilton seems to me very good. If I can ever be of any service to you in any way I hope you will call upon me! I am so sorry that you and Eleanor are not to be with us on the 10th, and it is very nice, very considerate and very fine that your Mother is to be here. We shall drink [to] your very special health in liquor your Aunt Annie has kindly provided! (Keep this to you). I am leaving for Washington this afternoon to return Friday noon next the day before the wedding. Accept my greetings and sincere love. Your affectionate Uncle Frederic[30]

Delano's advice can, of course, be taken at face value, and at face value it is altogether good advice. Uncle Fred's counsel can also be read against what would become an intense struggle for the future of Franklin. Uncle Fred's sister, Sara, wanted her only son to return to his stamp collection, his books, and his naval prints at Hyde Park, where she could lovingly look after him, much in the same manner that she had tended to her sickly husband, James, at the close of his life. This attitude did not prevail with Eleanor, Howe, and clearly Uncle Fred. Perhaps they already knew that to keep Franklin's spirit alive would involve keeping his mind (and body) alive as well. Daughter Anna would later note, "Both father and mother had to contend with my father's mother, who was vociferous in her demands that her only son resign himself to the life of an invalid and decide to live the life of a so called country gentleman at our Hyde Park home."[31]

But before those plans could crystallize, Franklin had to get off the island. The logistics of his transportation were vexing. How to get him to a train without painful jostling? How to keep the press from seeing him in such a prostrate condition? And, how could Roosevelt travel between Campobello Island and New York City if local authorities suspected him of being contagious? Dr. Lovett solved the last problem with a medical certificate stating that Franklin would not pose a health risk. As to the first problem, Uncle Fred overruled Howe's insistence that Franklin be transported back to the city by boat; instead, he had secured a private railroad car that would meet the party in Eastport, Maine. Some painful jostling would be unavoidable. Once that decision had been made, Howe went into action to solve the second problem. After the route had been decided upon, Howe strategically misled the assembled press at Eastport as to where they would be making land to catch the train. And so on the morning of Tuesday, September 13, thirty-four days after leading his children in a day of merriment and activity, they watched their father as he was taken out on a makeshift stretcher, six men maneuvering him across the family's property. To his worried children he called out, "'Don't worry, chicks, I will be all right.'"[32]

Howe's distractions worked flawlessly; just as the stretcher was being loaded onto the railroad car, the journalists arrived. Franklin turned his head and smiled. Howe had lit a cigarette and placed it in the new holder he had just given Franklin. Duffy, the family's sixteen-year-old Scottie, curled up on Franklin's chest. The image of a smiling, smoking man had a salutary effect. The *New York World* reported, "'Mr. Roosevelt was enjoying his cigarette and said he had a good appetite. Although unable to sit up, he says he is feeling more comfortable.'"[33]

Before the harrowing departure from Campobello, the family had warned Franklin to keep mum on the subject, not of his health generally, but on the dreaded "I" word. His half brother Rosy advised, "I don't think anything should be said about infantile until you are safely in N.Y. and am warning all those who know, including Ma, to that effect."[34] Franklin followed orders, but with his arrival at Grand Central Station on Wednesday, September 14, Louis Howe could no longer control the story. Dr. George Draper, a Lovett protégé, finally informed the press of the real cause of Roosevelt's health maladies. It was not a heavy cold, nor was it pneumonia. On Friday, September 16, Howe must have been stunned upon glancing at the *New York Times*. There, above the fold, in large bold type, the headline screamed, "F. D. Roosevelt Ill of Poliomyelitis." Others were also stunned.

Woodrow Wilson's son-in-law and perennial Democratic presidential candidate, William Gibbs McAdoo, wrote immediately to Roosevelt: "I am deeply grieved to hear from the morning's papers of your continued illness. It came as a great surprise to me as I had supposed that your recovery was complete."[35] Others, who, like McAdoo, had clearly been buoyed by reports in the *New York Times* and elsewhere, expressed similar sentiments.

Perhaps the one person who was actually pleased with the *Times*'s story and coverage was Franklin Roosevelt. That very afternoon Roosevelt dictated a note to the *Times*'s publisher, Adolph S. Ochs: "'While the doctors were unanimous in telling me that the attack was very mild and that I was not going to suffer any permanent effects from it, I had, of course the usual dark suspicion that they were just saying nice things to make me feel good.'" But, kidded Roosevelt, "Now that I have seen the same statement officially made in the *New York Times* I feel immensely relieved because I know it must be so.'"[36] Roosevelt did indeed have good reason for optimism—if he was reading only the *Times*. In its front-page story, the newspaper quoted Roosevelt's new doctor at length. Dr. Draper was clearly in lockstep with the family as to the severity of the virus: "'You can say definitely that he will not be crippled. No one need have any fear of permanent injury from this attack.'"[37] This rather astonishing public pronouncement of his patient's health—keeping in mind that the virus had not yet run its course—was strongly influenced by Louis Howe, who, according to Frank Freidel, was successful in getting Dr. Draper to temper his initial diagnosis.[38]

Apparently Dr. Draper was mouthing the party line, first established in Lovett's diagnosis at Campobello on August 25. It was then that Dr. Lovett had relayed to the family "'that complete recovery or partial recovery to any point was possible.'"[39] Dr. Lovett's initial optimism was tempered a week later. Recall that on August 31, a somewhat frantic Dr. Bennett had written to Dr. Lovett in the hope that he might assuage some of Franklin's fears. In response to that request, Dr. Lovett wrote, "The atrophy amounts to nothing, but any considerable loss of power in the legs should *not* occur. There is a progressive type [of infantile paralysis] but it is not like this as a rule, and I am not worried unless the loss of power is really marked and rapid."[40] But on September 16, the real extent of disability was still very much unknown. The reason for the uncertainty was that Dr. Draper wanted to allow more time for Roosevelt's body to heal from the acute stage of the illness. In a letter to Dr. Keen dated September 26, Eleanor relayed the news of the frustrating status quo: "The soreness is not yet gone so no treatments have been begun and Dr. Draper has just been keeping him very quiet in the hospital to give his muscles, legs and back a chance to recover."[41]

Most likely, Eleanor had not been privy to the letter Dr. Draper had written to Dr. Lovett just two days prior. It was a very different-sounding diagnosis than the one that the public had read on September 16. Regarding FDR's body, Dr. Draper reported, "'There is marked weakness of the right triceps; and an unusual amount of gross muscular twitching in the muscles of both forearms. He coordinates on the fine motions of his hands very well now so that he can sign his name and write a little better than before. The lower extremities present a most depressing picture.'" The news was equally ominous for Roosevelt's fragile emotional state. "'He has such courage, such ambition, yet at the same time such an extraordinarily sensitive emotional mechanism that it will take all the skill which we can muster to lead him successfully to a recognition of what he really faces without crushing him.'"[42] Perhaps Dr. Lovett had been too optimistic after all, for "a considerable loss of power in the legs" had occurred, to say nothing of muscles in the back and arms. By November, Dr. Lovett had conspicuously dropped the role of medical prophet as he reported to Dr. Bennett that their famous patient "'has come out of that state of nervous collapse in which all these cases find themselves for some little time after the acute attack'"; more importantly, he "'has done exceedingly well ever since his arrival [in New York] although the progress has been slow.'"[43] Again, Dr. Lovett seems to have been fudging, for as Roosevelt was finally discharged from New York Presbyterian Hospital on October 28, his chart read "not improving."

Just as uncertain as Franklin's medical future was his political future. For someone who had only recently learned to sit up in bed, the road back to the rough-and-tumble world of electoral politics must have seemed light-years removed from his bedroom on East Sixty-fifth Street. That uncertainty was poignantly captured by Lily Norton, a family friend of the Roosevelts, who visited with Sara in November. To Helen Whidden she wrote, "Tragedy rather overshadows this once happy and prosperous family, for Mrs. R's only son, Franklin Roosevelt, was struck down in August with a terribly serious case of infantile paralysis. He is only 39—both too old and too young for such a fell germ to disable him. He's had a brilliant career as assistant of the Navy under Wilson, and then a few brief weeks of crowded glory and excitement when nominated by the Democrats for the Vice Presidency. Now he is a cripple—will he ever be anything else?"[44]

Would he ever be anything else? That question clearly gnawed at Sara Roosevelt. Her son, with the assistance of Eleanor and Louis Howe, set out immediately to answer that haunting question.

3   Quo Vadis?

ALTHOUGH THEY KNEW THAT FRANKLIN ROOSEVELT might always be a cripple, Fred Delano, Louis Howe, and Eleanor Roosevelt made sure that it was not the only thing he would be, much to Sara Roosevelt's initial consternation. Franklin's political factotum, Howe, more than anyone else, would see to it that "the boss," as he liked to call him, would remain an active presence in Democratic politics at both the state and national level. Infantile paralysis was merely a minor setback, a stumbling block, so to speak, on the same career trajectory that Franklin so admired in his famous cousin, Theodore. Already, in the early 1920s, FDR and Howe planned a run for the New York governorship, and then, perhaps in 1936, a run for the White House. But before Franklin could do anything of a public and political fashion, he needed to relearn his own body—what it could and could not do now that the acute stage of the disease had passed.

That Franklin set his sights immediately on walking, or on giving the appearance of being back on his feet, is attested to in Eleanor's letter of November 13, 1921, to Dr. Keen. Home just two weeks, her husband was, Eleanor reported, "up in his wheel chair twice daily for several hours and I think his general health is gradually improving."[1] It would only be a matter of days, she believed, before Franklin would have enough strength to use his crutches with the aid of leg braces. Walking, of course, could do nothing for Franklin's political abilities; it could do everything for his electoral abilities. And so beginning in the autumn of 1921, Franklin embarked on what would be a five-year odyssey to learn to give the appearance of walking. That odyssey, as we will document, was at times a very public one, for if Franklin could not convince the average voter of his fitness and vitality, then he was through as a politician. He would script his spots most carefully, such that the media's and thus the nation's attention was focused squarely on his active, able, and controlled body. A public misstep in any of his premeditated performances could literally mean the end of any electoral prospects.

At this point in his recovery, though, Franklin was nearly three years away from his first important public and political performance of his body. Thus his recovery began textually, typically with Roosevelt dictating and Howe or Margueritte "Missy" Le Hand writing. Many of these early letters bear the direct imprint of Uncle Fred's "good attitude and character" advice of September 4. Perhaps Franklin's epistolary optimism represented his attempts to reclaim his own body, or perhaps it was a form of mental therapy. Beyond the obvious psychological benefits of this letter-writing campaign, however, is a pronounced rhetorical motive: to convince all who would listen that Franklin was on the way to complete and total recovery.

The instances of Franklin's outward optimism at this early stage are many. In a letter of June 19, 1922, to Dr. Keen, Franklin reported that he had just returned from a two-week stay in Boston, where Dr. Lovett had examined him and where he had also been outfitted with new leg braces: "My health has become remarkably good and I can now negotiate steps. I am glad to say that Dr. Lovett finds all the muscles working and all of them growing more powerful daily." Even more remarkable was Franklin's pronouncement that "in every other way I am entirely normal and, in fact, in better health than I have been for years."[2]

To the casual reader/voter, Franklin would seem to be the picture of health and vitality, hardly the cripple that he now was. Less than a year after his illness, Franklin had incorporated a very deft rhetorical touch in talking about his body, one that bordered on prevarication. For example, Franklin could negotiate steps by sitting and hoisting his body with his arms, one step at a time. He would never "walk" up a flight of stairs—not even with the aid of crutches. Franklin's muscles, particularly in his back and arms, were growing more powerful. His leg muscles, though, would never improve. And, with the extended exercises he was now taking, Franklin was no doubt healthier "in every other way." At this point in his convalescence, it is clear that the smallest improvements, the slightest gains, and any new means of locomotion were internalized and later "externalized" as signs of recovery.

Shortly after this letter to Dr. Keen, Franklin discovered what he felt to be an important breakthrough in his recovery, one that would occupy him for much of the remainder of his life—hydrotherapy. Perhaps keenly aware of the timing, on August 10, 1922, the one-year anniversary of his illness, Franklin reported the discovery to Dr. Keen and George Draper. "During the past six weeks I have been swimming three times a week," Franklin reported to Draper. "The legs work wonderfully in the water and I need nothing artificial to keep myself afloat."[3] To Keen, "For the past month I have been swimming three times a week, and the legs work perfectly in the water." He closed with what was now becoming a rhetorical staple: "In every other way I am entirely normal."[4] Franklin's early experiment and enthusiasm for hydrotherapy would later result in lengthy trips to south Florida and his development of a dilapidated resort in Warm Springs, Georgia. But it was not just hydrotherapy that Franklin found helpful in his recovery; along with warm water, the sun seemed also to give him strength. In a letter dated October 17, 1923, to fellow polio sufferer and Dutchess County resident Paul Hasbrouck, Franklin's optimism was unmistakable: "I have found for myself one interesting fact which I believe to be a real discovery, and that is that my muscles have improved with greater rapidity when I give them sunlight." Franklin reported to Hasbrouck that he was even more buoyed by a meeting he had recently had with a doctor who had informed him that "'there is one thing about this infantile paralysis which you may be sure of—you will get progressively better year by year until you die.' That," exclaimed Franklin, "is mighty encouraging!"[5]

There is an ironic downside, though, to Franklin's rhetorical optimism; it appeared to be working all too well. As early as January, 1922, the *New York World* reported that New York's famed Tammany Hall considered Franklin an ideal candidate for the U.S. Senate; moreover, the *Chicago Tribune* reported that many in New York considered him to be a good fit for governor. Some even expressed their belief privately to Louis Howe that Franklin would capture the party's presidential nomination in 1924. A correspondent named Thomas F. Durning reported to Louis Howe that "in a talk with Joe Tumulty [Woodrow Wilson's private secretary] he agrees with me that Franklin D. would be the party's best bet for president. . . . I am telling where it will be effective [as a] strictly inside story that when the convention smoke clears away Franklin D. will be the victor. Well it's a pleasant pastime and hope it could be realized."[6]

At this early stage of his recovery, and given the political winds aloft, Franklin actually felt compelled to invoke his health as a reason *not* to reenter the political fray. He wrote to the Democratic National Committee, for example, that "it is a matter of deep regret to me that my recent illness prevents my appearing before you at Chicago and talking this matter over instead of being obliged to resort to the extremely unsatisfactory method of presenting it in my correspondence."[7] Franklin had entered into a most important rhetorical dialectic: to close friends and family he was "in better health than in years"; to members of his own political party he was too ill even to travel, let alone to run for office. This dialectic, no doubt, would buy him the time that he and Howe had calculated. It would also buy him the time he needed to remaster his own body. In the meantime, Franklin's ostensibly contradictory views of his own health were beginning to enter the public sphere, and, not surprisingly, many of his enemies both within the Democratic party and without would fasten onto them.

If there was an initial public breakthrough in Roosevelt's political fortunes it occurred in June of 1924. Tammany Hall's Al Smith became a presidential contender in that year, and he asked the erstwhile politician from Hyde Park to be his campaign manager. At this point, the Smith campaign did not take Roosevelt as a serious threat; rather, they sought to gain from his family name and his good standing in the upstate region where the Catholic and anti-Prohibition Smith was viewed with some suspicion, if not hostility. This arrangement suited Roosevelt just fine since he was able to continue to expand his political contacts without being perceived as an incipient challenger to the popular New Yorker. Most importantly, Roosevelt was asked to deliver Smith's nominating speech. And while Roosevelt was not Smith's first choice, he very willingly obliged. Close to home at Madison Square Garden, Roosevelt's postpolio body would thus be heard and seen by a mass audience for the first time in nearly four years.

The nominating speech at the Democratic National Convention provided an exponential boost for Roosevelt. Although the "Happy Warrior" speech, as it would be known, was drafted for Roosevelt (by Judge Joseph M. Proskauer), his delivery and, more importantly, his presence highlighted his incipient physical and thus political comeback. Though the delegates saw him walking with difficulty on his crutches, they cheered him enthusiastically.[8] In order to deliver the speech, Roosevelt was carried to the platform in a wheelchair and then moved to the podium on crutches with the aid of his son James. It took Roosevelt a long time to reach the podium.[9] Cordell Hull, the chairman of the Democratic National Committee, stood close by just in case Roosevelt might stumble. Before speaking, Roosevelt asked Joe Guffey of Pennsylvania, who was seated next to him, to check the podium "'to see if it will surely support my weight.'"[10] What the immediate audience and those listening at home did not know was that Roosevelt had spent many hours of practice walking an equivalent distance in his New York home.

The nationally broadcast nominating speech established Roosevelt as an orator of note. His delivery turned a text he did not produce into his own.[11] Though the changes he made to the prepared text were minimal and insignificant, Roosevelt's extensive use of the first person "I," especially at the prologue and epilogue, produced the impression that the speech text was indeed his. Roosevelt also mentioned his extensive travel "to visit every state of the Union."[12] The speech itself was an ode to Al Smith, the "Happy Warrior," whose integrity and hard work earned him the respect of the entire nation. (The moniker was taken from a Wordsworth poem, and Roosevelt personally objected to its inclusion.) Roosevelt recounted Smith's achievements as governor, his humble beginnings, and his struggle against religious bigotry.

The text also incorporated a number of references to fear and faith, specifically, that one must have faith, not fear. Asking people to support Al Smith as the party's presidential candidate, Roosevelt requested that people not fall "to the subtle encouragement of false fear," and he reiterated that "the solid democracy of this nation will stand without fear and without hesitation loyally behind the nominee."[13] Even though this speech was ghostwritten, in future speeches Roosevelt would make frequent use of this appeal to reject fear. It is quite possible that when Howe inserted the sentence into Roosevelt's first Inaugural Address—that the nation had "nothing to fear but fear itself"—he was already familiar with Roosevelt's inclination to use such an appeal.

The media's immediate reactions to Roosevelt's performance were encouraging but far from unanimous. The *Washington Star* reported on June 26, 1924, that "there was a touch of pathos reflected in the faces of many delegates who had not seen him since the San Francisco convention of four years ago. . . . Today, after months of suffering from paralysis, he literally had to be lifted up the staircase by two strong men, and his face was drawn and deeply lined."[14] The *Eagle News* reported on July 2, 1924, that his nominating speech, "which was praised almost unanimously . . . is said to have brought him into the limelight as a gubernatorial candidate."[15] Some delegates even suggested turning to the "Dutchess Man as Deadlock continues."[16] Louis Riley of the *New York Times* wrote in a private letter to Roosevelt on June 27, 1924, "Please accept my hearty congratulations on your address yesterday. It was an admirable summing up of the public career of a man whose popularity is a tribute to New York. . . . Our Governor had an able advocate in you."[17]

The *Louisville Courier-Journal* was more emphatic and particular in lauding Roosevelt: "There was nothing at the Democratic Convention more inspiring than the heroism of Franklin D. Roosevelt. . . . It was the nominator that loomed large in the picture, an invalid on crutches, perhaps in pain, who conquered the frailties of body by sheer power of will." They concluded with a metaphorical flourish: "The world abhors the quitter who in his full strength goes down [sic] and will not get up. It admires the man who fights to the last and dies with his boots on. Franklin D. Roosevelt showed that this was the stuff he was made of."[18] The Roosevelt-as-boxer metaphor would not be idiosyncratic; in fact, it would soon be adopted by some of his closest advisors. The staunchly Republican *New York Herald Tribune* even reported that "Roosevelt's appearance on the speaker's platform, robust and ruddy, and with ringing voice, gave such evident proof of his general health that those responsible for the boom effort [to nominate him] felt that his physical shortcomings would offer no insurmountable difficulty."[19]

Roosevelt's performative politics at the convention, though, did not have everyone convinced of his good health. "Delegates . . . had in their minds a picture of a young man in the flower of his manly vigor stepping briskly to the podium," noted Kyle D. Palmer, a journalist covering the campaign. "Today they saw him virtually carried there, crippled by the creeping inroads of infantile paralysis, and obliged to prop himself against the speaker's desk once he had been lifted to his feet."[20] Another journalist was even more unsparing in his succinct evaluation: "He is hopelessly an invalid, his legs paralyzed. Wheel Chair, crutches and attendants are with him wherever he goes."[21] It is difficult to imagine that these reporters were witnessing the same convention as the others, yet the polarized accounts of Roosevelt's body would not be limited to 1924.

While the convention augured well for Roosevelt, it was an unmitigated disaster for the party. The Smith and McAdoo camps deadlocked, and after two weeks and 102 ballots the convention compromised on the conservative former ambassador to England, John W. Davis. Roosevelt was one of the very few men in the party to emerge from the convention unsullied. Walter Lippmann, for example, hailed Roosevelt for attempting to bridge the gap between the McAdoo and Smith camps and because, with good spirit, he rose above faction, religious bigotry, and hatred.[22] As the floor manager of the convention, Roosevelt gained much respect for his political skills.

Based on his performance at the convention, many wished to see Roosevelt run for the New York governorship, arguing that "had his health permitted" he could "win in a walk."[23] Indeed, there already existed some public sentiment that Roosevelt might one day run for office. The *Washington Star* stated on August 9, 1924, that while Roosevelt would not be a candidate for governor "this year," "Mr. Roosevelt waits discarding of his crutches before re-entering politics."[24] Reports of his improved health appeared following the convention in several newspapers. The *New York Evening Post,* on October 18, 1924, reported that Roosevelt was "slowly recovering the use of his lower limbs for the first time since 1921" and that "Franklin D. Roosevelt indicated today that he might throw his hat into the Presidential ring within the next decade, if his cure should be complete."[25] The *Star* reported on October 29, 1924, that Roosevelt's health was "greatly improved" and that he was "prepared to enter the heat of political battle."[26]

Roosevelt's return to national politics, the type of politics that he aspired to in the future, was imminent according to some. One article stated that "the popularity of Franklin D. Roosevelt in the convention stood the test of all its bitterness. He was a gallant and generous figure at all times, and the sheer force of his personality did more to offset the unsportsmanlike and often brutal behavior of some of those in the galleries than any other man." Roosevelt, it continued, "was the ideal representative of the New York Democracy at its best and the visible evidence of Gov. Smith's liberal, generous and good-humored temper. There is no place the Democratic Party could offer Mr. Roosevelt which he would not fill with the greatest credit."[27] Roosevelt's exertions at the convention were described in characteristically optimistic and physical terms. "The [1924] convention was great fun," Roosevelt reflected, adding that it "did me no harm and has actually put more pep into my legs than I ever had before."[28] In later years, Jim Farley, a man who would play a pivotal role in getting Roosevelt nominated in 1932, was enamored of not so much what Roosevelt actually said but the way in which it was said: "The nation listened to a magnificent voice which combined the best features of the sounding boxes of Enrico Caruso and Patrick Henry along with the deep carrying quality of Big Ben."[29]

Roosevelt's convention appearance and speech also brought favorable mail. Frank W. Sterling wrote Roosevelt that "due to your association in this case [the campaign] I shall vote for the Governor [Smith] this fall" and that "the high plane of appeal that you gave to the work added a lot to the Governor's prestige and this will be shown should he be a candidate in 1928."[30] Jerry B. Sullivan wrote to Roosevelt to congratulate him on his "magnificent address nominating Governor Smith. . . . It was not only excellent and eloquent, but filled with that spirit which carries conviction."[31] J. Frederic Tams of New York City wrote in his letter to Roosevelt, "I was at the convention yesterday, saw your face and manner, particularly the former and heard the matter, hence the foregoing outburst."[32] And Jedediah Tingle of Brooklyn, New York, wrote a telling letter: "I have always admired you—though not your politics; still, as you strode the streets of Washington your fine athletic figure always seemed to comport with the class you showed in all your doings and misdoings under Wilson's singularly mismated administration,—combinations of brilliancy and mediocrity, consecration to principles, and consecration to political pelf." Yet Tingle recounted, "when I listened to your scholarly measured words at Madison Square Garden, your character took on a new glory, the glory that can only come through the soul[']s conquest of pain and mental suffering, and I said, His very crutches have helped him to the stature of the Gods. This was exemplified by the fact that, bar none, yours was the outstanding figure at the convention." Beyond this single correspondent, Roosevelt's convention appearance "established you in the respect, admiration and affection of all America."[33]

A Mr. Joseph Valentine of Cincinnati, Ohio, wrote Roosevelt that his speech pleased him very much and that the speech "was not only a warm friendly tribute that you paid to him but a master address on Governor Smith's ability to lead the Democratic party at the coming election. . . . You told us you were not an orator, well I can only say that you have underrated yourself. It was a splendid nominating speech, the memory of which I will always remember."[34] Roosevelt replied to Mr. Valentine, "I am glad that you liked my speech. If it was a successful effort, I think it was because I merely said what I thought, and it came from the heart rather than from the head."[35] Roosevelt took the credit for a speech he did not write, but at the same time he presented a humble and honorable character.

After listening to Roosevelt's nominating speech over the radio, Francis Wilson of the Kansas City Railway Company wrote to Roosevelt, indicating that he "clearly and distinctly heard every word, even catching the intake of your breath and an occasional slight clearing of the throat. . . . It was a magnificent effort."[36] And James Wilson of Cincinnati wrote to Roosevelt, saying that "nothing would give me greater satisfaction, four years from now to have you restored to perfect health, and to see you the nominee for the Presidency, and to help you win the election."[37]

Some letters to Roosevelt were somewhat expedient but telling. Arthur Van Rensselaer wrote Roosevelt on July 21, 1924, after hearing his nominating speech via radio: "You proved yourself to be quite the hero of the convention." Mr. Rensselaer also tried to interest Roosevelt in purchasing an Automatic Electric vehicle as a "convenient means of getting about independently."[38] Roosevelt answered him on July 29, 1924: "The Convention seems to have done me good, and my legs are rapidly improving. I expect to spend part of the summer down at the beach, and fear that I would have little use for one of the automatic electrics for the present. If, however, I am not able to get rid of my crutches by next spring, I think I shall have to have one."[39]

To another well-wisher who also raised the issue of his health, Roosevelt wrote, "I have no doubt the doctor you mention is a splendid one, but the truth is that I have made such excellent progress under the course of treatment I am at present taking that I expect before long to be able to discard my crutches entirely, so it would not therefore be wise for me to try anything new at present, however well recommended."[40] To a professor who studied Hindu remedies and offered Roosevelt his special treatment for polio, Roosevelt wrote, "I am making such excellent progress under the treatment I am now taking that I hope before long to be able to discard my crutches, and under these circumstances it would not be wise for me to make a change."[41]

The secretary of the Louisiana House of Representatives, Irving Washburn, wrote to Roosevelt on July 11, 1924:

> I am wandering [sic] if you are really aware of the affectionate admiration for you which is very general in the whole country and in fact universal among those who have had the opportunity of meeting or seeing you. I have heard it on every hand during the trying days of the convention

from men and women from many states. Your really great speech and magnificent fight for Al Smith deepened and broadened this already well-developed sentiment toward you. . . . Of course, we are all greatly disappointed that the Governor was not nominated;—and after it became fairly obvious that he could not win, I had much company here in hoping for your name at the head of the ticket. One of your enthusiastic admirers said to me "Hell it's not legs we want in the White House! It's brains."[42]

In his reply to Washburn, Roosevelt wrote, "It will not be very long, according to the doctors, before I shall be really back in the game, legs and all. Of course having to use crutches at present is a considerable handicap, but I hope to be able to throw them away presently, and be active physically as well as mentally in future campaigns."[43]

Spurred on by his appearance at Madison Square Garden and the generally favorable reaction it engendered, particularly among the New York newspapers, Roosevelt went back to the hard work of making good on his word to "throw away his crutches." But in addition to the swimming, the massage, and the hours in the sun, Roosevelt revealed in a letter written shortly after the convention that his recovery was also about mind over matter—or, as Fred Delano put it, attitude. Upon receiving a letter by S. R. Betron, a disciple of Emile Coue, a Frenchman who advocated a mind-over-matter approach to physical ailments, Roosevelt wrote back, "In a way I have been following Coue['s] methods ever since I got this fool disease three years ago—I have been perfectly definite in my determination to throw away the crutches." But Roosevelt was not about to give up on the exercises, particularly the swimming. In the same letter, he detailed his plans for the fall: "In October [I] am going down to Warm Springs, Georgia, where there is a huge outdoor pool of warm water which gushes from a hillside."[44] Roosevelt had been informed about Warm Springs and its thermal spring waters by George Foster Peabody, a friend and Wall Street banker who had told him at the convention of the case of Louis Joseph, a young polio sufferer who had experienced a tremendous improvement in his locomotion while immersed in the resort's large pool.

Roosevelt arrived at Warm Springs on October 3, 1924. He would die there nearly twenty-one years later. In between, Roosevelt would experience some improvement. His optimism was such that he was initially convinced that he had found the place to cure infantile paralysis. He wrote as much to his mother: "I feel that a great 'cure' for infantile paralysis and kindred disease could well be established here."[45] And in a letter to his friend Hasbrouck back in Dutchess County, Roosevelt urged him to visit: "My month down there did me more good than anything I'd done before. . . . You feel wonderfully after staying in [the pool] for several hours and [you] can do a great deal of exercising."[46] More importantly, Warm Springs would be the place for mental improvement and for building his inner strength and faith. Once he discovered its potential personal (and thus political) value, Roosevelt quickly got involved in the administration of Warm Springs and its conversion into a center for polio treatment. In 1924, the resort was owned by Peabody, who leased it to Tom Loyless, a former editor of the *Atlanta Constitution.*

Warm Springs received national exposure on October 26, 1924, with the *Atlanta Journal*'s syndicated story, "Franklin D. Roosevelt Will Swim to Health." The article described the exercises Roosevelt took and the positive attitude he had with respect to regaining his health. The spring water and the sun were described as having a healing power, not to cure patients from polio but to "overcome the effects of the disease."[47] This article persuaded many to make the difficult trip to Warm Springs, to seek a remedy, and to enjoy the company of other polio sufferers. Though not of his own doing, this article was one of the early public relations successes that helped Roosevelt claim his slow recovery.

Roosevelt had never been known to be a particularly patient man, and his lack of patience was evident in his efforts to walk again, preferably without the clumsy and heavy leg braces. He was not content solely with the waters at Warm Springs, as attested to in a letter to Dr. Draper. While he was vacationing at Howe's summer cottage at Horseneck Beach, Massachusetts, early in the fall of 1925, Roosevelt wrote, "I had Dr. William McDonald look me over. Net result, he told me he could have me on my feet without braces. I accepted the offer and came here August 25th [1925]." Ever the optimist when it came to the prospect of walking, Roosevelt added, "I don't hesitate to say that this treatment has done wonders—so much so that I can now get within a very few pounds of bearing my whole weight on my legs without braces."[48] Just a few months later, his daughter Anna was privately less sanguine about her father's prospects for walking, or for Dr. McDonald's methods. She wrote to her mother, "Ma, it's awfully hard to tell whether Father is walking better or not. He doesn't walk very much, and doesn't exercise over much. . . . He is entirely 'off' Dr. MacDonald [*sic*] now—says he was ruining his legs—might get him to walk but would deform his legs."[49]

Yet despite his slow progress, Roosevelt's frequent statements to friends, allies, and the press about his recovery bore political fruit. The overall perception, coupled with press reports, helped Roosevelt to appear healthy and to claim credibly that he was back on his feet. To his friend, Abram I. Elkus, ambassador to Turkey in the Wilson administration, who suggested that he run for governor in 1926, Roosevelt wrote, "'You and I have been hit by germs so similar that our cases are in many ways parallel, and I am perfectly convinced that if you and I devote another two or three years to overcoming our disability, we will be in much better shape to render service than if we were at this time to enter actively into a campaign.'"[50]

But the health issue was not the only reason to avoid a run for political office. Roosevelt sensed that 1926 was not the best year to run, given the turmoil in the Democratic party, so he maintained an active political presence primarily by writing to many Democratic leaders. In his letters he solicited their input for improving the standing of the Democratic party, especially the progressive agenda that Roosevelt championed. Polio, historian Frank Freidel argues, had given Roosevelt the time to think and to write, to read many books and talk to many experts, thus allowing him to advance his political objectives and to expand his network of contacts without appearing unseemly.[51]

His disability, his struggle for rehabilitation, and his Warm Springs physician-like experiences were also transformed into rhetorical outlets. One such outlet was metaphor. In an editorial for the *Daily Telegraph* of Macon, Georgia, Roosevelt used an early medical metaphor to make his point: "The federal Civil Service needs a doctor" in order to "allow the most capable employes [sic] to rise and to allow the least capable employes [sic] to return gracefully to private life."[52] "Doctor Roosevelt," as he later would fancy himself, would make use of this rhetorical strategy in many future speeches.

With the continued Smith-McAdoo deadlock, some began to focus on Roosevelt as a presidential candidate for 1928. Roosevelt could not have been happier with such speculation. By now he was perceived by some as suffering from a temporary disability that would gradually improve and that walking was possible in the future.[53] He even felt confident enough to reject calls that he run for the Senate, claiming that "there are two good reasons why I can't run for the Senate next year [1926]. The first is that my legs are coming back in such fine shape that if I devote another two years to them I shall be on my feet again without my braces." The second reason was "that I am temperamentally unfitted to be a member of the uninteresting body known as the United States Senate. I like administrative or executive work, but do not want to have my hands and feet tied and my wings clipped for 6 long years."[54] Running for the Senate would limit and constrain his presidential aspirations, to say nothing of his vigorous body. In any event, senators did not become presidents, at least not in Roosevelt's time.

Howe was so worried about the attempts to draft Roosevelt in 1926 that he wrote to him about a possible political scenario: "I have been warned of a plan to get you to make a speech and then demand you to accept the nomination by a stampeded convention with everybody yelling 'We want Franklin.' This is, of course, a possibility, but I hope your spine is still sufficiently strong to assure them that you are still nigh to death['s] door for the next two years." Howe's ironic advice was to "please try and look pallid and worn and weary when you address the [1926] convention so it will not be too exceedingly difficult to get by with the statement that you[r] health will not permit you to run for anything for 2 years more."[55] To Roosevelt's good fortune, Al Smith and others took him at face value as a crippled man who, at best, could serve as a patron of the party but who could not hold office. But the rhetorical dialectic of health and sickness was still very much in place. In a letter to old Dr. Keen detailing his Warm Springs experiment, Roosevelt also detailed his own recovery: "I, myself, am coming along splendidly and can walk with only one brace. In other words, this whole disease is, in nine cases out of ten, merely a question of progressive improvements if you live long enough and don't falter."[56]

Though Roosevelt seldom spoke publicly from 1921 until 1928, he was not above giving speeches to small audiences. One such speech, titled "Whither Bound?" (from the familiar Latin phrase "Quo Vadis?"), offers a telling look at Roosevelt's state of mind and how he viewed and how he thought his audience (the 1926 graduating class of Milton Academy) might perceive the future. It comes as close as any personal or public statement by Roosevelt during this period to an acknowledgment of the attitude he had adopted in his own convalescence. At this stage in Roosevelt's life, we surmise that his speechmaking was not prone to the influence of speechwriters. We assume that he wrote this speech, and thus its content, theme, rhetorical strategies, and metaphors are the products of his own pen. "I would speak chiefly of the future," declared Roosevelt at the outset, posing the rhetorical question: "Quo Vadis—Whither Bound?"[57] The title already signaled the physical activity of walking. The only question left to be answered was "where?" But it was clear that Roosevelt would lead the way.

The context of the speech was the growing uncertainty and unrest throughout the world. But these conditions, Roosevelt explained, were "caused as much by those who fear change as by those who seek revolution; and unrest in any nation or in any organization, whether it be caused by ultra-conservatism or by extreme radicalism, is in the long run a healthy sign. In government, in science, in industry, in the arts, inaction and apathy are the most potent foes."[58] Roosevelt did not shy away from progressive thinking and considered it, at least theoretically, "a healthy sign." In other words, the one who thinks anew and unlike many others is healthy.

Roosevelt called for action and for active participation in human affairs. He also asked that unrest not be viewed only as unwarranted and threatening. The changes and the progress in many fields were caused by people willing to take risks. He said that the world could ill afford to have each nation cling to its own traditions and reject change, and he asked that people instead "discuss without fear, problems and methods formerly mentioned only by wild-eyed visionaries."[59] What was needed was progress and a willingness to admit the benefits of progress. Progress, stated Roosevelt, had been the way of science, especially medicine. Thus, no longer was an epidemic seen as an act of God but a solvable problem that could be identified, isolated, and cured. An epidemic such as polio, we might infer, was not first and foremost a problem for the moralist.

Roosevelt diagnosed the progress made through the centuries and highlighted the major achievements in improving human life, but he also pointed to recent unwarranted developments and their causes and potential solutions. These solutions he asked the graduating class to realize and, consequently, to adopt so that they might have faith in a better future. "I see many rays of pure light in that future," intoned Roosevelt the prophet. "I see not merely materialism—new inventions, new conditions, new words: I see something spiritual coming to you who will take part. Service to mankind . . . True service will not come until all the world recognizes all the rest of the world as one big family. To help a fellow being just because he is a fellow being is not enough. We treat that help too much as a duty, too little as an interest." It is hard not to read this statement as autobiographical. Roosevelt, of course, had experienced that help and service for the better part of five years, and he would rely on others for the rest of his life. He sought to motivate his young listeners by articulating a responsible and progressive political philosophy that called for social awareness and an end to the "disease known as 'class consciousness.'"[60] His medical metaphors were also early rhetorical proclivities that he would develop in later speeches, and his optimism was distinct and uplifting, precisely what a graduating class during troubled times needed to hear. But was Roosevelt speaking metaphorically? We should remember that the disease that had crippled him was understood as a disease of the lower classes.

The man who had earlier wondered aloud whether God had deserted him concluded that, instead of the cry of "the older days . . . 'Hail, Caesar, we about to die salute you,'" there could be an alternative: "Can we of to-day and of to-morrow, reverent in our purpose, strong in our hope, say, 'Hail, Lord, we greet Thee, we about to live.'"[61] The disabled ex-politician was all about optimism and a better future. The aspiring politician who could not walk had, by the close of the speech, answered his own question—"Quo Vadis?" The graduates of Milton Academy would walk with their speaker toward a better future.

By 1927, Roosevelt had additional room for optimism; talk about Roosevelt for president was growing quite loud.[62] In June, the Boston News

Bureau, under the subheading "An Active Sick Man," sought to refute any allegations that Roosevelt did not possess the requisite energy for high office. It was a strategy that Roosevelt would frequently appropriate over the next five years.

> Illness of a lingering sort usually drives from the ordinary man all thoughts of work. The activities of some of our nationally known "sick men" would make Samson weaken. Witness the activities of Franklin D. Roosevelt, former assistant secretary of the navy. The opinion prevalent in some places that the illness of infantile paralysis which he acquired in 1921, after his campaign for vice-presidency of the United States, and from which his recovery is rapid and certain, must in some way limit his efforts is readily dispelled by intimate knowledge of his varied and active interests. Apart from the position he holds in political circles, he is an active member of the New York law firm of Roosevelt & O'Connor and a director and general vice-president in charge of [the] New York office of Fidelity & Deposit Co. of Maryland, the second largest surety company in this country. Either one of those positions would be sufficient to keep the ordinary man fully occupied. But Mr. Roosevelt does not stop there,—he is also president (and an active one) of the following: American Construction Council, Georgia Warm Springs Foundation, Meriwether Reserve, Inc., and Boy Scout Foundation of New York City; and he is a trustee in these: Vassar College, Seamen's Church of St. John the Divine, Holland Society, Naval Historical Society, Fifth Avenue Hospital, and also chairman of the following: Taconic State Park Commission and of the Committee on Study of Real Estate Mortgage Bond Companies, and others too numerous to mention. The indefatigable barrister and publicist is keenly interested in naval history, prints and pictures. Incidentally, his collection of naval pictures is generally conceded to be one of the finest in this country.[63]

Among clippings gathered by Paul Hasbrouck, a newspaper article stated that "Mr. Roosevelt was an appealing public figure before his affliction. Three years ago when he addressed the Democratic national convention at Madison Square Gardens [1924], he was able to stand only by the aid of crutches, to put the name of Governor Smith in the running for the presidential nomination. Now Mr. Roosevelt has discarded his crutches; a brace and a cane is all he needs to lead his active life."[64] The campaign to appear healthy and fit had begun to bear fruit, and Roosevelt could not have been happier with such newspaper accounts.

As a part-time resident of Warm Springs, and later as founder and owner of the Warm Springs Foundation, Roosevelt improved the appearance of his Georgia spa and replaced some of the dilapidated buildings with newer ones. He purchased a farm nearby and sought to be a successful farmer. He also built a little house and named it the "Little White House." Was it named so because of presidential aspirations? Sara Roosevelt testified it was not.[65] Yet health and politics would become a permanent pair in Roosevelt's lexicon. Perhaps Roosevelt knew where he was going all along.

4 In Sickness and in Health

AL SMITH AGAIN SOUGHT THE PRESIDENCY IN 1928, and Franklin Roosevelt again was asked to give the nominating speech. Again he accepted, but his loyalty to Smith was drawing to a close. Unlike the situation in 1924, Smith received the party's nomination in 1928, and on the first ballot. Four years after his last convention appearance, and after continuous exercise and therapy, Roosevelt now impressed nearly all in attendance, including the press, with an improved ability to walk. The cumbersome crutches had been replaced with a cane and the strong arm of one of his sons, typically James. Roosevelt's locomotion involved dragging one foot and then swinging the hips to bring the other leg forward. Leg braces held each leg locked in place, giving Roosevelt the appearance of standing or walking. The upper body was erect and the upward jut of the jaw radiated energy and vibrancy. With this technique mastered in the fall of 1926, Roosevelt presented himself no longer as a crippled man but instead "was determined to show himself . . . as a man merely lame."[1]

Roosevelt's new body performance was auditioned at the Democratic National Convention in Houston, and it clearly impressed Richard V. Oulahan of the *New York Times:* "Crippled in body and limb, that picture of him changed quickly as his voice rang out with a clarity and strength that carried it across the acres which Sam Houston Hall covers. Pink cheeked, full of glow of health, Mr. Roosevelt offered an attractive appearance."[2] Another New York journalist, Will Durant of the *New York World-Telegram,* was moved to eloquence by Roosevelt's presence at the convention. Durant began by writing that Roosevelt was "'beyond comparison the finer man that has appeared at either convention. . . . A figure tall and proud even in suffering; a face of classic profile; pale with years of struggle against paralysis; a frame nervous and yet self-controlled with that tense, taut unity of spirit which lifts the complex soul above those whose calmness is only a stolidity; most obviously a gentleman and a scholar.'" Durant continued his encomium: "'A man softened and cleansed and illuminated with pain. . . .

Hear the nominating speech; it is not a battery of rockets, bombs and tear-drawing gas—it is not shouted, it is quietly read; there is hardly a gesture, hardly a raising of the voice. This is a civilized man; he could look Balfour and Poincare in the face. For the moment we are lifted up.'"[3]

The election year of 1928 would prove to be more "uplifting" than even Durant might have imagined. Because Smith was running for president, he wanted someone he trusted to succeed him as governor—a loyal person who could help him secure the votes of New York's forty-five delegates. Roosevelt had the name, the clout, and the respect, and he was not a Catholic; thus, he could balance the vote. But Roosevelt refused to run in 1928, at least initially. Roosevelt and Howe figured that 1928 would be a Republican year, so they insisted that his planned recovery was a major limitation. Roosevelt was "definitely, finally, and irrevocably out."[4] The dialectic of health and sickness was once again front and center; however, the dialectic would be exacerbated by Roosevelt's initial reluctance to run for the governorship in the fall of 1928 when he cited his health as an impediment. Some of the major newspapers in the state would later point to the health excuse as a reason for their readers not to vote for him.

In the late summer of 1928, Roosevelt retreated to Warm Springs, content to let Al Smith select someone else to succeed him in Albany. But Louis Howe was worried. In a September 25 telegram to Roosevelt, he detailed the "expected squeeze" for a Roosevelt candidacy, since "both sides want to compromise on you." Howe was strongly opposed, and he urged Roosevelt to wire party leaders "a definite final and irrevocable statement that your health will not permit you to run." By the telegram's close, Howe was emphatic: "My conviction that you should not run is stronger than ever and Eleanor agrees with me in this. There is no answer to the health plea but any other reason will be overruled by the Governor himself."[5] Roosevelt could not have missed the irony: Nonelectoral salvation was premised on his fragile health.

The following day, Howe sent yet another telegram to Roosevelt, asking him again to "get a definite wire up here immediately or you will have no peace in Warm Springs."[6] Still no answer, or wire, from the boss. Back in New York, the Smith forces were clearly turning up the pressure on a besieged Howe. Again he wired Roosevelt, this time with the nonhealth-related reasons why he should not accept. First, "you are not the kind of man who would take a job and leave it to an understudy." Smith had wrongly figured that Roosevelt might prefer to be a governor in name only. And second, "I do not believe your running will really induce anyone to vote for Al, but on contrary some of your friends now voting for Al for your sake will vote for you and not Al if you run." He closed the telegram with a final plea: "As I wired yesterday situation will get exceedingly strained unless you definitely and irrevocably decide one way or another. Please let me hear from you."[7]

Roosevelt's silence was feeding a great deal of gossip back in New York, which Howe relayed back to him: "Several papers tomorrow will say that you are absenting yourself from New York during convention so that you would be drafted in your absence and that you really intend to run after you have been sufficiently persuaded." Howe's understanding, what he had been telling other journalists in order to avoid such unseemly speculation, "was that your doctors had declared your further improvement made your services as Governor impossible for the next two years."[8] By September 28, Howe was still nonplussed as to Roosevelt's intentions. He continued to urge him to make a "direct statement . . . for publication that will settle the matter."[9] At this late date, it is clear that Roosevelt was intrigued by the possibility of becoming governor. Maybe, just maybe, the legs were ready for the campaign trail. By October 1, Al Smith had gotten involved in the "draft Roosevelt" movement afoot at the party's state convention in Rochester. Instead of sending a telegram, Smith was on the telephone to Warm Springs, trying to locate the coy Roosevelt. Howe was perfectly aware of Smith's intentions. "'Beware of Greeks bearing gifts,'" he advised Roosevelt.[10]

On October 2, Howe finally got the statement for which he had been pleading. In a telegram sent to Smith, the *Elmira (New York) Advertiser* reported, Roosevelt told the presidential candidate that "'my doctors are very definite in stating that the continued improvement in my walking is dependent on my avoidance of cold climate and on taking exercise here at Warm Springs during the cold winter months.'"[11] But Smith did not relent. He got the able administrator Herbert Lehman to run for lieutenant governor and the wealthy John J. Raskob to underwrite Roosevelt's financial stake in Warm Springs. Despite Howe's strenuous objection, Roosevelt finally agreed not to turn down a convention nomination.

The *Elmira Advertiser* reported on October 3, 1928, that Roosevelt agreed to run for governor to help the cause of the "Beloved Governor." It also reported that "Roosevelt's name was the most discussed, although it was generally felt by the delegates that his physical infirmity due to an attack of infantile paralysis a few years ago would prevent his entrance into the campaign."[12] Al Smith finally got his man, or thought he did. Roosevelt had now to turn a disadvantage into a golden opportunity.

Roosevelt had only four weeks to campaign for office and against Republican assertions that he was unfit and "dangerously ill."[13] Such assertions were founded, in no small measure, on Roosevelt's earlier statements in which he initially refused the party's nomination. In fact, the day after his nomination the *New York Herald Tribune* opined, "Let the desperation of the Democratic cause in the nation and in this state be conceded. Who can defend the risking of another's health and whole future career in the cause of one's own vanity and ambition[?] The nomination is unfair to Mr. Roosevelt."[14] To attempt to counter the health-related concerns raised by Roosevelt's initial refusal to run, Smith told a press conference that "'Roosevelt was mentally as competent as ever in his life,'" and that "'a Governor does not have to be an acrobat. We do not elect him for his ability to do a double back-flip or a handspring.'"[15]

Roosevelt mounted an energetic campaign that, with hindsight, would be a useful dress rehearsal for the presidential campaign of 1932. His campaign strategy in countering the health issue "was to display himself frequently and vigorously to the electorate of New York."[16] And this he did with unusual energy. Out on the hustings, his body would be the most compelling proof.

Roosevelt was interviewed by reporters on October 9, 1928, about his campaign strategy vis-à-vis the issue of his health. When a reporter suggested that "it [the active campaign] is a rather ambitious program, I would say for a man . . . ," Roosevelt completed the hesitant question, "who can't get around." The questioning continued: "Don't you think that you will be somewhat on the defensive in regard to that telegram you sent to Rochester that your health would not permit you to . . ." Roosevelt again interrupted the reporter. "I don't think so, if people *take a look* at me." The reporter was not yet satisfied. "I know that. But I am asking in regard to the telegram. How can you reconcile that?" The candidate explained, "There is no reason why I shouldn't continue while I am in Albany to take a certain—a certain amount of exercising for the leg muscles." The need to maintain his exercise routine was also touched upon with the implication that too many trips to Warm Springs would disrupt his duties as governor. Roosevelt countered that it was not necessary to go to Warm Springs for exercise but that "probably, instead of going, as the Governor has in the past, to Atlantic City, after the 30 day bills are over, I may run down to Georgia for two or three weeks."[17] To the assembled press, Roosevelt was not only walking, he was now running.

Asked a day earlier about his state of optimism, Roosevelt replied jokingly that "'most people who are nominated for the Governorship have to run, but obviously I am not in condition to run, and therefore I am counting on my friends all over the state to make it possible for me to walk in.'"[18] And "walk" he did—all over the state, riding in the backseat of an open-canopied car, standing (by holding a metal bar installed in his car) at every election stop to deliver a short speech. Between his acceptance speech on October 16, and November 3, 1928, Roosevelt's travel itinerary was ambitious: Binghamton, Deposit, Port Jarvis, Hancock, Owego, Elmira, Corning, Hornell, Wellsville, Olean, Salamanca, Elmira, Dunkirk, Buffalo,

Batavia, Rochester, Canandaigua, Seneca Falls, Syracuse, Oswego, Watertown, Boonville, Rome, Utica, Herkimer, Schenectady, Troy, Albany, Flushing (Queens), New York City, Bronx, Yonkers, New York City again, Brooklyn (Academy of Music), and finally, Madison Square Garden. The two-week "show-and-tell" motoring campaign throughout the state included overnights at local hotels where more receptions, short addresses, and meetings were scheduled.

Before Roosevelt hit the road to make himself as visible as possible to the New York electorate, Louis Howe helped put together a small political pamphlet titled "The Facts of the State Campaign." Perhaps predictably, Roosevelt's brief biography was chock-full of not-so-subtle allusions to the candidate's good health. The first sentence set the tone: "Franklin D. Roosevelt has laid down one of the most active careers in business and the professions to become a candidate for Governor." The second sentence was more specific and emphatic: "The manifold activities of politics will mean no increased strain on the splendid energy which he has employed so constantly with no diminution since the attack which eight years ago deprived him to a great extent of the use of his legs."[19] With frequent use of terms such as "active," "activity," "energy," "useful," and "hurried," to say nothing of FDR's purported naval duties during World War I, Howe was clearly attempting to quell doubts about the candidate's health.

On the first day of the trip, in Binghamton on October 17, Roosevelt alluded to his extreme mobility: "Everywhere that I go, whether it be in the South or in the Middle West or New England . . ." and "I spent many weeks during that campaign [1919–20] going up and down the United States, clear out to the Coast, down South, up in New England."[20] The prepolio and postpolio periods were joined to portray an able-bodied candidate who energetically traveled to every corner of the country. At one point, Roosevelt even wished the campaign could be extended from a few weeks to three more months so he could counter what he had "noticed in a fairly extensive trip around the country"—a most un-American assault on religious liberty.[21] Roosevelt was appalled to find during his travels the prejudices toward Al Smith's Catholicism. Though the focus was religious bigotry, Roosevelt subtly sought to impress his auditors with his extensive travel, his tuning in to public sentiments throughout the country, and his willingness to engage in a long fight for religious liberty—all acts of a vigorous candidate.

The stop in Salamanca on October 19 was typical. Roosevelt made references to his relationship with the crowd and with individuals he had known for quite some time; he reminded his audience of his past travels throughout the state and how happy he was to see them; and he made fun of Republicans as he stated that "it was a shame to draft me." He retorted in kind: "Well, for a man who deserves sympathy, it seems to me that I am pretty husky." Roosevelt did not address the issues of the campaign, stating that they were well known. He made one final reference to his physical ability in the subtle form of reminding his listeners of his extensive travel "up and down the United States a good deal of late."[22] Relating to people and establishing a bond, coupled with his disarming and ironic approach to his health, were keys to Roosevelt's traveling campaign. The major legislative issues were left for larger venues. Roosevelt, of course, had good reason to focus on his health since his initial refusal to run now had to be countered, even contradicted.

On the same day, in Jamestown, Roosevelt again addressed his fitness for office: "Do I look to you good people like an unfortunate, suffering, dragooned candidate?" he asked. "We started—the Democratic State Ticket and I started, day before yesterday, from Jersey City, and since then, commencing with Orange County, we have spoken in every single county along the Southern tier. That is pretty good for an unfortunate invalid and a lot of other cripples." Roosevelt continued, "We left Elmira this morning by motor, and we have had six outdoor meetings today. So I hope you will pardon me if my voice is a little bit frayed tonight. That is the only part of me, except a couple of weak knees, physically, but not morally."[23] In the evening, at Wellsville, Roosevelt continued the ironic refutation regarding attacks on his health: "You know, some of my Republican friends around New York are talking about the kind of sympathy that the people of the State ought to have for this unfortunate invalid who is running for Governor (applause), and I don't think that any of us need worry about that."[24] Rhetorically, Roosevelt did not shy away from the health issue, and he attempted to refute any lingering doubts with his very presence as proof of his fitness. Thus did the oral and the embodied merge on the campaign trail.

Roosevelt was also fond of using his proximity to past military activities to lend him the necessary physical cover. He told his Buffalo audience on October 20 of his trip ten years earlier to Château-Thierry, following the advance of the American army: "I go back to a day in particular when several miles behind the actual line of contact between the two armies . . . as we went through these fields there were American boys carrying stretchers, and on those stretchers were German boys and Austrian boys and American boys being carried to the rear." The point Roosevelt made was about the lack of discrimination among the wounded soldiers during World War I, in comparison to the prejudices against a presidential candidate who happened to be Catholic. He concluded by emphatically stating that "if there is any man or woman who has seen the sights that I have seen . . . [and] after thinking of that, can bear in his heart any motive in this year which will lead him to cast his ballot in the interest of intolerance . . . 'May God have mercy on your miserable soul.'"[25] Roosevelt skillfully resorted to a useful scene also to push the subtle point about his active military experience and his direct engagement with warfare and its carnage. In addition, he condemned prejudice of any kind, which also subtly included the disabled. Intriguing within this scene is Roosevelt's healthy body against the backdrop of wounded and disabled soldiers.

Many in the media appeared to be persuaded by the motoring campaign. The *Times of Batavia (New York),* under the heading "Fine Character of Roosevelt Wins Support," reported on October 27, "The chorus of approbation following the Roosevelt selection has been varied by only one discordant note. It was the protest of two or three leading opposition journals against what they were pleased to call the selfish drafting into party service of a man who has not yet fully recovered from the effects of a serious physical disability." The *Times of Batavia* could not abide such discord: "This rather forced, and by no means sympathetic, objection is now in the way of complete abandonment." The article also stated that Roosevelt's own reassurances regarding his health left the newspaper to declare that it "cannot imagine a rational citizen of this state withholding his vote from Mr. Roosevelt."[26]

The following day a reporter asked Roosevelt, "The trip has been a pretty hard one so far. I wonder how you feel, how you have stood it?" Roosevelt replied punningly, "I am *standing* it extremely well" (emphasis added).[27] In Rochester, on October 22, Roosevelt for the first time used the issue of his own disability to stress election objectives. "I may be pardoned," he began, "if I refer to my own intense interest in the care of crippled children, and, indeed, of cripples of every kind. . . . From the practical dollars-and-cents point of view, it is obvious that if a large proportion of these cripples can by proper treatment be restored to active and useful citizenship, the money spent on them by the State will come back many times through their increased productiveness." Economic sense, rationalized Roosevelt, mandated care for crippled individuals. But there were other reasons for such care: "there is the great humanitarian side of the subject. I have seen," continued Roosevelt, "thousands of examples of crippled adults and children, who by proper care have been restored to normal life."[28] His own suffering might have turned Roosevelt into a genuine humanitarian and compassionate person, but for successful persuasion he knew he had to resort to a tangible argument. The evidence to merit an investment in crippled people was physically present, standing before them:

> I suppose that people readily will recognize that I myself furnish a
> perfectly good example of what can be done by the right kind of care.
> I dislike to use this personal example, but it happens to fit. Seven years
> ago in the epidemic in New York, I came down with infantile paralysis, a

perfectly normal attack, and I was completely, for the moment, put out of any useful activities. By personal good fortune I was able to get the very best kind of care, and the result of having the right kind of care is that today I am on my feet. And while I shall not vouch for the mental side of it, I am quite certain that from the physical point of view I am quite capable of going to Albany and staying there two years.[29]

The purpose of this statement was clear: Roosevelt was cured of his earlier affliction and was now ready to become governor. This talk of the right care, curing, and of course the "perfectly normal attack" implied that he had recovered and was therefore fit to assume office. He was standing on his own two feet, and that was "proof" of his recovery. The physical and visual were convincing proof regardless of the misrepresentation of his disability.

His rhetorical efforts continued to bear fruit with local newspapers. The *Daily Messenger* of Canandaigua reported that Roosevelt was on his way to Buffalo "after a vigorous three day appeal to the strongly Republican southern tier of New York."[30] The following day, the same newspaper carried a photograph of a standing Roosevelt casually leaning on a table. It indicated that Roosevelt gave a short speech from his car and that "men and women crowded around Mr. Roosevelt's car and for several minutes there was much handshaking and pow-wowing. The candidate smilingly spoke a word of greeting to those who were able to get near him."[31] The photograph that the *Daily Messenger* used was clearly not taken during the local event covered, and no photograph of a standing Roosevelt could be located in the Roosevelt Presidential Library collection.

On October 23, the *Syracuse Journal* reported that "Mr. Roosevelt has been receiving enthusiastic receptions upstate."[32] The topic Roosevelt raised was water power, and it was here that he attacked his opponent, Albert Ottinger, for his stand on this issue. "As he concluded his attack," the newspaper reported, "Mr. Roosevelt was given a loud demonstration by the crowd. He is a good campaigner and many times during his speech was able to key the crowd up to enthusiasm. His long experience in campaigning had taught him how to emphasize an insignificant point sufficiently to bring a demonstration."[33] More significantly, there was no mention of his disability.

In Utica, Roosevelt did much rhetorical activity with his legs: "As I have been going around this State . . . ," "That is where I stand," and "I want to go down to Albany, and I am going down to Albany, to carry out the greatest constructive program for good government in modern times."[34] His appearance must have left a deep impression, as the *Utica Observer-Dispatch* reported: "Those about the hotel, who had previously met Mr. Roosevelt, were surprised at his appearance when he walked into the lobby last evening. Upon his former appearance here, seven or eight years ago, there were expressions of sympathy for the man who possessed the ambition to be about with the apparent physical affliction he suffered." That visage differed dramatically from the one Roosevelt now presented. "He was at that time," the article continued, "unable to walk and plainly showed in his facial lines the effect of his suffering. He has not only gained in flesh and general appearance since then but is able to walk fairly well. He says he feels well and rather enjoys the work of the campaign, strenuous though it be."[35]

At times the health issue was addressed head on and with mild sarcasm. It was at Syracuse that Roosevelt opened his speech by stating, "'Well, here's the helpless, hopeless invalid my opponents have been talking about. I have made fifteen speeches today. This will be the sixteenth.'" Cheers followed.[36] A similar jab was made in Troy on October 26: "Republican editorial writers in the State of New York," Roosevelt said, had asked the following: "Isn't it too bad that that unfortunate man has had to be drafted for the Governorship? Isn't it too bad that his health won't stand?" Roosevelt, who had by then been on the campaign trail for ten days, responded, "Too bad about this unfortunate sick man, isn't it?"[37]

The *Times of Batavia* discussed Roosevelt's health on November 3. Note that "their" pronouncement was a direct appropriation from the candidate's campaign brochure drafted by Howe: "Franklin D. Roosevelt has laid down one of the most active careers in business and the professions to become candidate for governor. The manifold activities of politics will mean no increased strain on the splendid energy which he has employed constantly with no diminution since the attack which eight years ago deprived him to a great extent of the use of his legs. . . . Energy and useful activities marked Mr. Roosevelt's career from the very beginning."[38]

Roosevelt's physical presence was a tool—perhaps *the* tool—of the political campaign. The press focused on his health largely because Roosevelt had made it an issue with his initial refusal to run, and he responded by displaying his best walking ability and an uncanny visual presence around the state. Historian Alfred B. Rollins argues that Roosevelt "had to fight off the burgeoning propaganda that he was an unfortunate, physically incompetent victim of political exploitation. It would be all too easy for the public to believe his own frequently asserted claims that he was not ready for office yet."[39]

Yet talking about his health and standing before a live audience was quite different from showing photographs of his disability. When Roosevelt arrived at Hyde Park to cast his vote on November 6, he asked the many newspaper and newsreel photographers not to picture him being carried from the car. His wishes were respected and the illusion maintained.[40] Clearly, Roosevelt was concerned about the political impact of his health. He was so concerned that he even drafted an entire campaign address on the issue of his health. "I am deeply touched at the tender solicitude displayed by my Republican adversaries," he wrote, "first as to my anguish of mind, and now as to my feebleness of body. I trust I have convinced them that the martyr's crown was not being pressed upon my head." The candidate continued, "I would like at this early date . . . to reassure them as to my physical condition. Let me soothe their fears by explaining that the impossibility of indulging in excessive physical exercise has enabled me to take far better care of my health than is the case of most men as actively engaged in business as I have been for the last four years."[41]

Roosevelt's creative refutation bordered on sarcasm. "My family physician has found me a very poor customer," he continued. "Let me assure them again that my only physical disability which is a certain clumsiness in locomotion and which I trust will eventually disappear, has interfered in no way with my power to think. . . . I pride myself that during the past four years, I have done rather more than the average man's daily stint."[42] Roosevelt's strategy had always been not to deny his disability but to modify its appearance, to argue its temporary nature, and to dialectically deflect the most severe accusations with sarcasm and irony—and with his own apparently healthy body.

Finally, Roosevelt threw the ball back to the Republican camp; he would "gladly furnish any of the Republican campaign managers with proper weekly bulletins containing respiration, temperature and general physical condition. There is one disability I have which I imagine particularly impresses the Republican leaders of the Legislature as being very serious." Roosevelt had to confess "that no man, compelled to move somewhat slowly, is a very good dodger. For the last four years these gentlemen have spent most of their time dodging issues, dodging responsibility, dodging, rather poorly, the verbal missiles of Governor Smith and I have been grieved to note, quite frequently dodging brickbats thrown in brotherly strife at each other."[43] This speech, we surmise, was never delivered. A handwritten note on the speech draft reads "not used." Was this speech too sharp an attack? Could it backfire, or was it simply unnecessary given the generally positive newspaper accounts of his trip? Or was it, perhaps, a master text from which Roosevelt could extemporize as needed?

One of the final campaign addresses was delivered on November 2, at the Brooklyn Academy of Music. The speech was both a tribute to Al Smith and an appeal for voters to focus on the issues and not on the speaker's health. Roosevelt recounted his extensive travel "into every corner of our own State. . . . We have been out along the Southern Tier of counties of this State, out to Lake Erie, then up to Buffalo, and back by way of Lake Ontario, through the middle of the State." What for an average politician would be considered a mundane rendition, for Roosevelt's audience meant fitness and assurances of future ability. Roosevelt's final plea to New York's electorate was for people to vote "not for my health, but for my comfort (applause), I want a Democratic Legislature with me."[44]

But Roosevelt's health was not simply a partisan issue that appeared only in Republican newspapers. Even the usually friendly *New York Times* editorially advised against a vote for Roosevelt. "A noble character, a devoted public servant, a man of the finest instincts, highly cultivated," the editorial began, "what a shame that in his poor condition of health he has been called upon to make such a sacrifice!" If only the Democrats had waited another two years, "then all of us independents and Republicans would have been delighted to vote for him, but this year, as you see, the thing is sorrowfully impossible for us."[45]

Despite the influential *Times*'s ambivalence, Roosevelt won a very close race to become New York's governor, just as Al Smith had hoped. But Smith lost the presidential election in a landslide to Roosevelt's old friend from the Wilson administration, Herbert Hoover. Roosevelt's victory was nothing short of remarkable, however; in a little more than a month he had proven many persons wrong, even some in his own party. Infantile paralysis had not won. By mastering his own body, by laboring tirelessly for its recovery, he had turned the most important corner in his life. Now he could joke about his health without the terseness and edge of the campaign. When a man named Charles Ritz, whose company sold arch supports and foot "appliances," wrote to the governor-elect about his health, Roosevelt made some playful notes on the semiliterate letter. To the question, "Can you walk without a cain [*sic*]?" he responded, "I cannot walk with a CAIN because I am not ABEL." To the question, "Have you any pain below the hips?" he wrote, "My principal pain is in the neck when I get letters like this." To the question, "Does both your shoes fit you even?" he quipped, "They fit me EVEN unless by accident I put on an ODD shoe." And to the question, "Are you sure of your step?" Roosevelt scribbled, "We all have to watch our step with so many prohibition agents around."[46]

Reflecting on the campaign years later, campaign staffer Jim Farley offered a very Rooseveltian view of campaigning and the candidate's health. "I think FDR had reserves, spiritual and physical of which he had no realization until political contest brought them out," he explained. "While I am not qualified to express a medical opinion, his re-entry into politics was the greatest therapeutic event. . . . He could deliver more punch sitting down than Teddy Roosevelt standing up."[47] Farley would return to the boxing allusion.

On January 1, 1929, Roosevelt delivered his Inaugural Address as the governor of New York. Some of the themes were straight out of his "Quo

Vadis?" message to the Milton Academy graduating class. A progressive agenda, for example, was described in terms of interdependence, "the recognition that our civilization cannot endure unless we, as individuals, realize our personal responsibility to and dependence on the rest of the world. For it is literally true that the 'self-supporting' man or woman has become extinct as the man of the stone age. Without the help of thousands of others, any one of us would die, naked and starved."[48] If Roosevelt was somewhat dependent on others it was because everyone, to one degree or another, was dependent on others, not just the disabled.

In this interdependent world, he continued, we "must give our time and our intelligence to help those who helped us . . . to aid those who are crippled and ill; to pursue with strict justice, all evil persons who prey upon their fellow man." The implication was that all were helped at some point and all needed to help, and the fact that some needed more help than others did not change the principal idea that all had an active role to play. Roosevelt's call extended his own motivation to help himself and others who suffered from infantile paralysis. The mobile governor was restless: "We have but started on the *road,* and we have far to *go,*" he stated (emphasis added).[49]

After Roosevelt had delivering the Inaugural Address, Dr. Leroy W. Hubbard of the Warm Springs Foundation told the press that "'Mr. Roosevelt is in fine general health and there is no question that if he keeps to the proper routine he will continue to improve.'"[50] But privately, Roosevelt had his fears. To Frances Perkins, his labor secretary, he said that initially he was not sure he could go through the campaign for governor, "'but I made it.'"[51] Indeed, the physical ease Roosevelt displayed in public was in stark contrast to the difficult and slow process of moving physically. Perkins and other cabinet members witnessed how slowly he moved and how difficult and painful his walking appeared to those waiting for him.

Roosevelt's gubernatorial win also accomplished what he and Howe had hoped: It commenced serious national exposure and speculation about a possible presidential candidacy. But the fall of the stock market and the ensuing depression would change much in Roosevelt's political calculations, including the fortuitous metaphorical juxtaposition between the disabled politician and a disabled nation. The possibility of a run for the presidency was slowly becoming a reality, and the strategy now was to make only vague and noncommittal references to any direct talk about presidential aspirations. Anything more specific could hurt him, as could too much publicity. Roosevelt stated, "'I want to *step on* any talk of that kind with *both feet.* That is colloquial but clear'" (emphasis added).[52] This statement was more than colloquial; it was the statement of a disabled person confidently presenting himself as physically "normal."

As governor, Roosevelt had to act carefully to assure the public of his ac-

tive governorship without taking on too many controversial issues, especially given the Republican control of the assembly. He also had to appear
to be building on Smith's record while also ensuring that he would not be
perceived as dependent on his predecessor. Smith believed that Roosevelt
was a figurehead, what Hoover would later call derisively a "trimmer," who
badly needed his advice. Nothing could have been further from the truth.
Roosevelt quickly established himself as a bright and energetic governor.
He began with an active agenda, seeking to balance the budget, implement-
ing farm reform, and proposing park improvement and judicial reform.

Roosevelt would learn much during his first term in Albany, including
the importance of his rhetorical skills. While his speeches were drafted primarily by Samuel I. Rosenman and Howe, Roosevelt would make extensive
changes when necessary to ensure that the final product clearly carried his
stylistic imprint. He also discovered radio and used this modern technol-
ogy to his benefit. Radio was a communication medium well suited for Roosevelt because it played up a resonant and assuring voice. Roosevelt had
both qualities. And it was a medium that did not require physical visibility;
imagery was left to the listener's imagination. The medium could come to
him and not the other way around. Roosevelt could use it in the comfort of
his home or his office. Regarding the use of radio, he opined that the old
"silver tongues" and old-fashioned oratory were replaced by radio; moreover, radio allowed a politician to bypass a partisan press. "'Whereas five
years ago ninety-nine out of one hundred people took their arguments
from the editorials and the news columns of the daily press,'" Roosevelt
said, "'today at least half of the voters sitting at their own firesides listen to
the actual words of the political leaders on both sides and make their decision on what they hear rather than what they read.'"[53] A modern, more disembodied approach to politics and governance was developing.

At Albany, Roosevelt quickly put forward a series of noncontroversial
policies, designed primarily for rhetorical effect. On February 28, 1929, he
asked a commission to study the need for an old-age pension; on March 4,
1929, he proposed a program to readjust the tax burden on rural school dis-
tricts and to guarantee minimum salaries for teachers; on March 12, 1929,
he called for a Saint Lawrence power commission; on March 16, 1929, he
requested $168,000 for three agricultural research studies; on March 20,
1929, he recommended a referendum on a four-year term for governor; on
March 21, 1929, he requested a commission to propose legal reform; on
March 22, 1929, he sent a message supporting several social service- and
labor-related bills; on March 25, 1929, he recommended the creation of
a public utility survey commission; on March 26, 1929, he recommended
the construction of hospitals and other state institutions at the cost of
$50 million. Only a few of these recommendations eventually passed, and
they were primarily Republican substitutes. But the active agenda of the

first few weeks and months was a strong signal of an active and energetic governor; it would serve as a useful precedent to the famous first one hundred days of 1933.

Roosevelt's activism early in his term did not persuade everyone of his vitality. When Roosevelt went to Warm Springs after the first few months in Albany, the *Elmira Advertiser* wrote that "'he was an exceedingly tired man,'" and that "'the office proves a severe tax upon his strength, for he is by no means well.'" Roosevelt decided to challenge the press report: "'I not only am but have been throughout this year and for several years past extremely well.'"[54] He also asked the editor of the *Elmira Advertiser* to correct the statement and to identify the source of this bad news, explaining that in several midwestern newspapers it was reported that he was on his deathbed. This newspaper article, and others like it, were detrimental to Roosevelt's political position, but he was quick to challenge them. With a dismissive and sarcastic tone, Roosevelt sought to "correct" any perception of physical weakness. He did not take a chance that his talk about his "mild" case of infantile paralysis or the usefulness of cripples in general would alone alter people's perceptions of the disabled.

The governorship was the platform for the next and ultimate task—getting elected president. Roosevelt engaged in a quiet campaign for reelection, touring, speaking, and extending his network of contacts. Despite bitter fights with Republicans in the state assembly, Roosevelt's first term was successful and reelection in 1930 was almost guaranteed. He was able to present accomplishments that could serve him nationally as well. And they did. In April, 1930, at a Jefferson Day dinner of the National Democratic Club in New York City, Roosevelt devoted his address to attacking the concentration of wealth. The other speaker, Burton K. Wheeler, a U.S. senator from Montana, declared afterward that "'as I look over the field for a General to lead the people to victory under the banner of a reunited, militant progressive party, I cannot help but fasten my attention upon your Governor. The West is looking to Roosevelt to lead the fight and with him I feel sure we can win.'"[55] This declaration was the first significant public call for Roosevelt's presidential candidacy.

In accepting his renomination for the governorship, Roosevelt stated that while two years earlier he "wanted to be a disciple in a great cause," this time he accepted the nomination "for the simple reason that I still march forward in that cause." As the presidential election neared, the need to "walk" and "march" would increase. Just as his predecessor had fought for the "ground of progress," so had Roosevelt fought "inch by inch" during the preceding two years. The struggle, stated Roosevelt, was not easy because the Republican leadership threw "every kind of wall and boulder . . . across our path."[56] The acceptance speech was distinctly about Roosevelt's achievements and contained the first-person pronoun throughout, coupled with active verbs: "I advocated," "I stressed," "I spoke," "I recommended," and "I am confident."

And confident he was. While two years earlier, Roosevelt "visited every part of the State," this election, he could not give much thought to the campaign as he was needed in Albany to prepare the executive budget. Roosevelt also mocked his opponent, the Honorable Charles H. Tuttle, for stating that he would go upstate and "get down among the people." "I know," stated Roosevelt, "that the people will be properly flattered at his condescension, his descent from the high heights he occupies."[57] The very language Roosevelt used to "prove" his vigor and stamina he also used to criticize and patronize his opponent.

Belying Roosevelt's outward confidence of reelection was a new campaign, orchestrated by Howe, to dispel once again rumors about Roosevelt's poor health. Initially, Howe's public relations campaign advertised that a $250,000 insurance policy had been issued on Roosevelt's behalf and was accompanied by a medical examination report. Later, a much more publicized $500,000 life insurance policy was issued. Dr. E. W. Beckwith, the medical director of the Equitable Life Assurance Company, also issued a very public report testifying to Roosevelt's excellent health—both moral and physical.[58] Roosevelt and Dr. Beckwith were interviewed by the press on October 18, 1930, when the life insurance policy was issued.

Dr. Beckwith stated how pleased he was "to see such a splendid physical specimen as yourself, and I trust that your remarkable vitality will stand you in good stead throughout your arduous campaign." Though the reelection campaign put the governor "under very great strain," Dr. Beckwith stated that Roosevelt "passed a better examination than the average individual." Dr. Beckwith also opined that "the moral hazard in the thing counts for a tremendous amount in getting a large amount of insurance. A man who doesn't lead a clean, decent life, even though he passes the examination physically, will be turned down. The moral hazard enters into it almost as important as the physical."[59] In other words, Roosevelt may not have been completely healthy or cured of his illness, but he was a moral person. For a disease that was often associated with uncleanliness, the lower class, and the morally bankrupt, Roosevelt did not fit the pattern. Dr. Beckwith medically exonerated his patient from that perception.

Roosevelt contributed to the press interview with his account of his involvement in Warm Springs. He enthusiastically elaborated on the healing power of the warm spring waters and of his initiative to bring polio victims to the facility. Roosevelt's narrative took an active form: "I took these people and we fixed up a cottage for them. I got the local doctor. . . . I put them in the pool. . . . I went down there and discovered that the American

Orthopedic Association was holding its annual meeting in Atlanta. I went up to the association meeting. . . . I took a year's lease, an option on the property. I came up to Albany."[60] Roosevelt did all of that. He was already healed and now was fit enough to be active in helping others to achieve the same. Perhaps even more important than the actual insurance policy was the newspaper coverage that it generated. Clearly, no sick man or degenerate's life would be insured to the tune of half a million dollars. As we will detail in chapter 7, the suasory force of this life insurance policy was not limited to the 1930 gubernatorial election.

Roosevelt loved to campaign, and as soon as circumstances permitted he resumed his travel in the state. The campaign speeches increasingly included references to the national situation. In Buffalo on October 20, he charged that, while the stock market plunged, "not one single step was taken by the responsible officials of the national [Hoover] Administration to put on the brakes, or to suggest even that the situation was economically false and unsound." Roosevelt went further, suggesting that "if Washington had had the courage to apply the brakes the heights to which the orgy rose would not have been so high, and as a result . . . the fall from the heights would not have been so appallingly great."[61]

Roosevelt was now sitting in the driver's seat, ready to navigate a better road. His attack was specific; he criticized the administration for concealing the extent of unemployment and "as conditions became worse, the messages of good cheer became more and more optimistic." While thousands of working people were discharged, the administration issued statements attesting to the fact that "things were getting better."[62] Roosevelt, who understood better than many the power of faith and optimism in overcoming despair, chided the president for having the very same approach. Roosevelt did so precisely because his optimism carried more credibility than the president's. Once the depression discredited Hoover, Roosevelt only had to continue the discrediting. He could not go wrong there.

Indeed, in the same address Roosevelt called on people to face the situation "honestly and bravely. There is no need for abject pessimism. . . . I have no doubt that capital and labor alike can, and ultimately will, put their shoulder on the wheel to pull our industry out of the deep mud." Roosevelt was riding smoothly, in control of the speed and the brakes, offering his help to those whose wheels got stuck in the mud. The implication was that the joint effort of a little push would get the car back on the road again. But Roosevelt had reasons for his confidence. Though the Republicans had controlled the New York state assembly for nearly twenty years, nothing was done to relieve people of "the staggering burden of taxation until I became Governor, and until I pointed out the way." Roosevelt lifted the weight of people by showing them the way. As with his "Quo Vadis?"

speech four years earlier, he pursued his road metaphor until the end of the address: "The path of our duty is clear. You and I know that as good Americans, we will manfully and bravely follow that path."[63] Roosevelt charted a new path and suggested that he was the better navigator—and certainly the more masculine.

In Rochester on October 21, Roosevelt concluded another campaign address, declaring, "I stand flatly upon my party's platform; and I assure you that all of the Democratic candidates are united in this position. There is no diversity or doubt among us. We stand together."[64] In Syracuse the following day, discussing electric power, Roosevelt told the audience that "as I stood on the banks of the St. Lawrence and Niagara Rivers and saw this rich possession which should rightfully belong to the people of our State . . . I formed a firm resolve that as long as I was Governor . . . no more would be given or leased to private corporations." Later in the same address, Roosevelt told his audience that he "personally went up to the St. Lawrence River . . . and personally inspected the sites on which we all hope the State will soon erect its huge power structures."[65] With his physical presence on the river banks and with his statement of resolve regarding electric power, Roosevelt conflated the symbolic and the literal to present himself as an active and determined governor.

Roosevelt won his second term as governor with a majority of more than 700,000 votes, and he achieved the impossible—carrying the heavily Republican upstate New York region. Freidel cites several factors that helped his reelection, in addition to his personal appeal: the depression, his successful courting of organized labor, the Republican split over Prohibition, the effective platform of the Democratic party, opponent Tuttle's weaknesses, and Jim Farley's new upstate organization.[66]

But there were other factors, too. Howe and Roosevelt had a campaign formula that was based on distributing daily news releases and generating form letters that were sent to many politicians and political activists around the nation. Howe's staff also read hundreds of newspapers, scrutinized their arguments and editorials, and compiled scrapbooks still intact at the Franklin D. Roosevelt Presidential Library.[67] Both Roosevelt and Howe paid close attention to the health issue and its coverage in newspapers around the nation. In a memo dated May 15, 1930, Roosevelt wrote Howe that he would not write a foreword to *The House of Miracles,* as the very title "is unethical from the point of view of every doctor in the country, and it is just this sort of thing that we have been trying to avoid at Warm Springs."[68] Though the reference is not altogether clear, the implication is significant. The title, presumably for an upcoming book, would give the impression that only miracles could cure infantile paralysis while Roosevelt had tried hard to convince many, including the medical profession, that treatment was warranted and that improvement was possible. Roosevelt was consistent in presenting himself as steadily improving due to sound medical treatment and not the result of a miracle, regardless of the truth.

As his refutation of the *Elmira Advertiser* suggests, Roosevelt and Howe were also quick to correct any articles that were misleading—even if it involved small, out-of-state newspapers. When the *Newark Call* wrote that "the indispositions and travels of Governor Franklin Roosevelt have resulted in giving Lieutenant Governor Herbert H. Lehman a prominence in public affairs," Roosevelt, through his secretary Guernsey Cross, fired back a letter on February 19, 1930, stating that "Governor Roosevelt had had no 'indispositions' and is in extremely good health." The letter urged that the false impression be corrected.[69] A similar letter was written by Roosevelt on December 18, 1930, and addressed to the editor of the *Danville (Virginia) Register.* Roosevelt protested a statement in that newspaper for claiming that his "health is still poor." "My health," he wrote, "is excellent, though as you know I still have to wear braces following infantile paralysis, but that can hardly be construed as having anything to do with general health."[70]

When the *New Orleans Morning Tribune* wrote on March 2, 1931, that "Governor Roosevelt suffered a tragic paralytic stroke which for a time incapacitated him, but in recent years his health seems to have much improved," Roosevelt's secretary found enough reason to respond.[71] He wrote to the editor, not for publication, flatly rejecting the reference to "paralytic stroke or stroke of any kind. In the epidemic of infantile paralysis in New York in 1921, Governor Roosevelt contracted that contagious disease, and there is absolutely no connection between infantile paralysis and a paralytic stroke."[72] The *Tribune* issued a correction on April 2, 1931, making a distinction between infantile paralysis and paralytic stroke. To this correction, secretary Cross wrote an appreciative thank-you letter, stating, "I fully realize the errors which oftentimes slip into news items unintentionally. The Governor's health is of the best and you can readily understand that he would not care to have any other impression go forth to the people."[73]

Roosevelt and his close aides left nothing to chance. They covered most media outlets to correct "false" impressions coincident with an elaborate media campaign that emphasized visibility and physicality. Underlying this active refutation of misleading newspaper accounts was a very basic motive: Roosevelt wanted badly to be president. So no newspaper was too small, no misstatement too trivial as he prepared for the next great challenge. That challenge would be met by much of what Roosevelt (and Howe) had learned at Albany.

Dark days in Hyde Park, 1922

FDR shortly after the "Happy Warrior" address, 1924

FDR on the beach in Florida, 1924

FDR "walking" his way to victory in 1932

FDR and Eleanor at the infamous Governors Conference dinner
at the White House, 1932

FDR and his mother in Hyde Park, 1933

5 Looking for Looker

AS HIS PRESIDENTIAL PROSPECTS gained momentum, Roosevelt and those around him were increasingly concerned with and preoccupied about the public's perception of his health. He was worried about what he described as "'a deliberative attempt to create the impression that my health is such as would make it impossible for me to fulfill the duties of President.'" He added that there were some who knew "'how strenuous have been the three years I have passed as Governor of this State, this is taken with great seriousness in the southern states particularly. I shall appreciate whatever my friends may have to say in their personal correspondence to dispel this perfectly silly piece of propaganda.'"[1] As we detail in this chapter, Roosevelt would aid and abet those friends.

Letters, many anonymous, spread throughout the country, some even suggesting that Roosevelt was incapable of governing not because of his polio or even from a paralytic stroke but because he suffered from syphilis.[2] To address the growing concerns about his health, a special campaign was put into action in order to "prove" Roosevelt's fitness and to attempt to dispel any lingering suspicions that he was not physically fit to be president. Roosevelt was now closer than ever to his dream of becoming president, and no doubt he was not going to allow his image as a vibrant and active politician to be dashed by a vicious whispering campaign.

While the 1932 Democratic National Convention was still nearly a year and a half away, Roosevelt's plans had crystallized to the point where he felt he needed to quiet some of the whispering. In some cases the whispering had become quite loud—and public—such as a statement by Mrs. Jesse W. Nicholson, president of the National Women's Democratic Law Enforcement League: "'This candidate, while mentally qualified for the presidency, is entirely unfit physically.'"[3] That Roosevelt had successfully quieted much of the whispering in New York in just two years was a testament to his well-conceived plan.

However, as talk of a possible Roosevelt presidential candidacy grew, the predictable rumors about his health resurfaced. These were national rumors. They needed a national response. Enter Earle Looker.

Earle Looker was a friend of the Oyster Bay Republican Roosevelts, the family from which Eleanor hailed. He was also a writer. Alfred Rollins suggested that Louis Howe may have been the one to mastermind what would transpire between Looker and Roosevelt.[4] Hugh Gallagher considered the entire arrangement "cooked up."[5] And Frank Freidel deemed it a "spectacular stunt."[6] The precious few elliptical primary sources in the Roosevelt Presidential Library indicate that a supposedly "innocent" medical review was anything but and that Roosevelt was directly involved in the arrangement to publicize this "objective" medical report, the aim of which was to give him a clean bill of health.

The preparations for such a project are most interesting. In a letter to Eleanor Roosevelt on December 16, 1930, Earle Looker wrote the following:

> Since my trip West, where I have been doing considerable sounding—and the sounds are quite vibrant enough, plans for the story have taken a great step forward. Working with my agent, John Gallishaw, I have been quietly looking about to find the best possible publisher for the particular thing we have in mind, one who is most likely to create the sort of organization we will need for fast and effective distribution of the book. . . . My backers understand exactly what I have in mind and why. Since they are so practically and enthusiastically for you and with me, assuring me I may have just as long as I need to do the very best work I can and insure my peace of mind in many ways, I feel less embarrassment than I otherwise might, in making one request of you in their behalf: That is that, while the Governor can at no time refuse information about himself and that he should of course not do so, that, however, until I am well underway with my story, it would be much appreciated if he would find it possible to discourage any extended work of which his personality—not policies—is subject. . . . As I read this last paragraph back, my dear Mrs. Roosevelt, I suddenly understand why diplomatic language seems so utterly impossible! The request, however, is simple enough; I have merely complicated it because of my intense desire not to make one false step in a matter that seems really very important.[7]

The plans for the medical report that would attempt to clear Roosevelt certainly involved Eleanor Roosevelt. Though the referent in the letter is vague and the backers unidentified, we can assume that the subject matter is a story, most likely an article and also a book written for quick publication and distribution. We can also assume that it was Eleanor who was Looker's principal contact in the "other" Roosevelt family. That she proved persuasive with her husband is attested to by what transpired in the summer of 1931.

The article Looker wrote about Roosevelt's health was published in

Liberty Magazine, a widely read weekly publication that fancied itself "A Weekly for Everybody." Before the issue containing the article hit news-stands on July 25, 1931, Louis Howe had already sent a copy of the article "to every county Democratic chairman in the country, and to any correspondent who expressed doubts over Roosevelt's health."[8] One of Howe's mailings ended up in the hands of Jim Farley, who was then completing a three-week trip to the West to sound out key party operatives as to a possible Roosevelt candidacy. On July 17, he wrote to Howe in his signature "flamboyantly Irish" green ink. "I read the Liberty Magazine article today," he began, "and think it is a corker. I think it is a mighty fine time to have it appear because it answers fully [a] question that was put to me many times during the past 3 weeks."[9]

That Looker and the Roosevelts were in cahoots on the story is suggested in a letter he wrote to Franklin on July 16, 1931. It begins, "Well sir, we got away with the 'Liberty' article despite all obstacles." Looker also described to Roosevelt the excellent circulation of the magazine. "Our story," he continues, "is the lead article in the magazine and is featured upon the cover. I think we can be sure that at least seven and a half million readers are sure you are physically fit!"[10] The strategy was clear—an extensive national distribution of an article Looker wrote testifying to Roosevelt's health and fitness to be president.

The story, provocatively titled "Is Franklin D. Roosevelt Physically Fit to Be President?" was indeed featured on the cover of the magazine's July 25 issue.[11] While the article, discussed below, contained written evidence testifying to Roosevelt's fitness for the office, the question raised by the title has a most interesting accompanying visual prominently displayed on the magazine's cover. As we noted earlier, physical fitness had an important corollary—that of masculinity. The more physically fit, in other words, the more masculine. And, of course, only fully masculine men were "capable" of doing politics in the public sphere. The question raised on the cover has its visual representation in two separate renderings. On the cover's background, in the upper left-hand corner, is an arresting image, given the subject in question: a man in street clothes is shown throwing (and landing) a right-handed punch, while another man reels backward to the ground, staggered from the blow. The logic of the cover suggests that a physically fit man can violently assault another man if need be—with his own fists. The physically fit man is in control of his own body, aggressive when needed, and capable of decisive, physical action on a moment's notice.

That boxing image, according to Farley, had a certain cultural, and thus political, capital at the time. The former New York State athletic commissioner colorfully detailed that appeal:

For F.D.R. to be deprived of the use of his legs was akin to depriving an eagle of his wings. The miracle—and miracle it was—that F.D.R.'s terrific heart won through; the wingless eagle flew and flew high. Now this gallant struggle must be taken in the context of its times. The American people were sports-mad. Nothing captured their admiration more than the "fighting heart" of a "fighting man." This was enacted on occasion in the ring at Madison Square Garden in a raw drama which the American people found most gripping. A great Champion would swing through the ropes into the ring to thunderous and idalatrous [sic] applause. But as the bell clanged, it would appear that something was wrong; the Champion was off form and getting a terrific lacing. As the rounds progressed, a breathless house would watch the C[h]amp, in the vernacular, "taking punishment." . . . Taking punishment is a progressive process; the more a man takes, the more he is unable to defend himself. Usually, at least one eye was closed, and the blood from his shredded face ran down over his chest to his shoes. Finally, nothing but his fighting heart would be keeping the Champion on his feet, when the smashing knock down punch came. Down would go the Champion; in the parlance of the Game, he had been "decked," and the count to ten which would deprive him of his title would be started over the fallen man. But sometimes a miracle would happen, a triumph of spirit over matter. The subconscious of the Champion would rouse his fighting heart. He would pull himself up and tear into his opponent with literally the blind fury of a badly wounded lion, and summoning the last sinew of his battered body, knock out his adversary. There was a phrase for this, the supreme of all supreme accolades in the sports world: "He got up off the deck and went on to win." F.D.R. earned that accolade, and as no other man in American history before or since even remotely approaches. Dempsey got up off the deck and went on to win against Firpo at the Polo Grounds and the country since has loved him and his image of a fighting American Champion. But that fight was on and over in four rounds, less than twelve minutes. But it was long and agonizing years, before F.D.R. knocked down by polio at Campobello in 1921, could get up off the deck in 1928 and four more years before he could go on to win in 1932.[12]

Perhaps the editors of *Liberty Magazine* were paying Roosevelt their highest compliments; here was a fighter performing for a "sports mad" public, and he was winning. Roosevelt had gotten "up off the deck" to defeat a most obstinate foe. Or had he?

If boxing metonymically stood in for bodily fitness and masculinity on the cover of *Liberty Magazine,* then the other image suggests a verbal fitness, but one that is perhaps still in question (hence the titular question, "Is

Franklin D. Roosevelt . . . ?"). On the cover's foreground is a larger image of a well-dressed young man with a young boy (presumably his son) hard by his right side. To their immediate left is a clearly impassioned police officer, haranguing the father with a menacing index finger. The young boy looks anxiously upward at his father. The visual suggests hostile, authority-based accusation. Whether the young man, a symbol of potentially imperiled patriarchy, can answer that accusation remains to be seen. As readers open *Liberty Magazine* to find the answer, they are greeted again with a more explicitly discursive appeal to Roosevelt's masculinity. In a subtitle, Looker promises, "A Man to Man Answer to a Nation Wide Challenge." That Roosevelt's political fitness is bodily based is clear: A "man" simply cannot be a "man" without a fit, functioning body. But Looker had also tapped into the other important issue for the prospective candidate in 1931—the challenge was national in scope. Presumably, then, a satisfactory answer would remove any global concerns about Roosevelt's fitness for office. And it was a satisfactory answer that Roosevelt (and Looker) provided.

Perhaps not surprisingly, after the article in *Liberty Magazine* was published, Looker himself became the focal point of press coverage. The *Springfield (Massachusetts) Republican,* presumably no fan of Roosevelt's, covered the story with the title: "Article on Gov Roosevelt's Health Brings Northampton Writer Bricks and Bouquets." The newspaper interviewed Looker and suggested that he was "hired by politicians to hush a whispering campaign, advised to spike the political ambition of a leader." It indicated that the article was supposedly "an impartial study of the physical fitness of the New York state executive and clean bill is given the man as a result of an examination by three of New York's leading specialists." The same newspaper also reported that "Mr Looker is sticking to his guns. He reiterates that he is [in] no one's employ, that writing is his business and the topic was dug up by him and by no one else." Furthermore, "Mr. Looker himself paid for the medical examination." For balance, the newspaper described Looker's connection with Theodore Roosevelt and his family. Also discussed was Looker's forthcoming book on Franklin D. Roosevelt, a book that Looker described not as "a pure biography . . . but . . . a study of the man and his traits." The newspaper interview ended with "a second emphatic denial that there was any financial compensation from Roosevelt, the Democratic party or anyone else."[13]

Looker was clearly pleased with himself and the interview because he sent Roosevelt a letter on July 20, 1931, enclosing the article from the *Springfield Republican,* "which may amuse you." The next sentence is most revealing: "The question of who paid for the physical examination was, and still is between us, frightfully embarrassing . . . but it had to be answered as I answered it" (ellipses are in the original). In other words, Looker did not pay for the medical examination; Roosevelt did. Looker also indicated to Roosevelt that "the story itself gives the sort of an interpretation we all most desire." He lamented that "while we can dramatize some things we really have nothing of a smashing kind that does not need to have the pumps working to keep it afloat. Those things, undoubtedly, you are reserving for the actual campaign after the convention." Looker advised Roosevelt that "this is the time to go into a prayerful silence to create something of dramatic importance which will provide grand copy before the Convention."[14] Whether due to Earle Looker's influence or not, Roosevelt did have "some things" of a "smashing kind" that he was saving for the convention and its aftermath.

Looker wrote Roosevelt again on August 12, 1931, informing the governor of their earlier discussion they had in Hyde Park about Roosevelt publishing several articles ghostwritten by Looker. Looker was also privy to a piece of information he gladly forwarded to Roosevelt—that of a plan to send journalist George Creel to interview Roosevelt on behalf of *Collier's*. Looker advised Roosevelt "to give no magazine interviews for a time and in the meantime let me get out enough copy under your own name to establish your own personal thought."[15]

Two weeks later, Looker wrote Roosevelt regarding the articles Roosevelt/Looker would write for the McClure Syndication. Looker reminded Roosevelt that "the fact that I am the 'ghost writer' is secret." What Looker had in mind was a monthly piece "on world affairs, rather than the U.S.," and that "Lloyd George is doing it for them in England, Herriot in France." Looker ended this letter with the following: "Merely 'the ghost' wishes to make the background as clear as possible, then fade into it."[16]

On September 5, 1931, Looker wrote Roosevelt a short note and attached a cartoon to make a point about their secret arrangement. "If, in conversation with someone or some group that will report it you said: 'NO, I DON'T WANT A REPORT—WE ALL KNOW THE CONDITION,' it would be grand stuff for later use," Looker wrote, closing the letter with "Faithfully, Marquis."[17] The cartoon in question depicted a king identified as Hoover holding a document titled "cause of crime." A criminal is sitting next to him with a gun pointed at King Hoover and a little girl standing in front of the impressively elevated king. The girl is identified as Wickersham, and several "reports" are spread on the floor. The caption reads as follows:

> "What do you know about his business?" the King said to Alice.
> "Nothing," said Alice.
> "Nothing WHATEVER?" persisted the King.
> "Nothing whatever," said Alice.
> "That's very important," the King said . . .

George Woodward Wickersham was Hoover's head of the National Commission on Law Observance and Enforcement, which focused primarily on

Prohibition. (He had also been President William Taft's attorney general.) The meaning of the cartoon was clear: Looker advised Roosevelt that it was very important to state, if necessary, that he knew nothing of any arrangement made between the two of them. Behind the constant advice he gave Roosevelt stood a frightened Looker, fearful of having his stunt exposed and his reputation ruined.

The very idea of Looker giving Roosevelt advice on what to say, or more precisely, what not to say, indicates that he did not know Roosevelt very well. This seeming lack of familiarity does not lend credibility to Looker, who was undertaking to write a biography of Roosevelt. Whatever arrangement Roosevelt had with Looker, it seems that Looker was quite taken by this contact with the presidential contender and felt that the secret deal allowed him both access and privilege of counsel. It also appears that the additional syndicated articles Looker had in mind did not materialize. Roosevelt had only one use for Looker: to publish a piece that would "prove" once and for all his fitness to be president.

In 1932, Earle Looker published a biography titled *This Man Roosevelt*.[18] "The object of this study," writes Looker at the outset, "is to isolate the truth from the propaganda piled up about this potent name, and to represent the man as he really works and relaxes, thinks and lives. Disregarding controversial political documents and the usual political-life narrative, politics plays no part in this report except where essential to give a clear view and an unprejudiced expression of his intimate traits of character, his mental and physical abilities and disabilities."[19] Thus begins what purports to be an objective account of a person many—most notably, Looker himself— wished to see as the next president.

The book, however, has neither footnotes nor any other form of source citation. It is essentially a public relations tract designed to promote Roosevelt's presidential potential and to reprint the "findings" of the *Liberty Magazine* article. The book is heavy with claims of impartiality, objectivity, and truthfulness, which, of course, suggest just the opposite. Looker begins (erroneously) with Roosevelt's illness on August 28, 1921, more than two weeks after the fateful days at Campobello. He indicates that the initial newspaper reports that Roosevelt had caught a heavy cold and that he was threatened with a bad pneumonia were misleading. He describes at length Roosevelt's impatient character and its importance in speeding his recovery and return to work. The first year of struggling with the paralysis already suggests a heroic Roosevelt who would win the admiration of his friends for his persistent efforts to regain his health.

Looker reports that in 1922 the medical profession considered the first twelve months after a polio attack to be crucial for some improvement, yet they recognized that no further recovery was possible. Indeed, he indicates that Roosevelt made no improvement in the first two years and that this lack of progress motivated him to begin swimming exercises, first in Florida and later at Warm Springs. The net effect of this early physical exercise was not an improvement in his leg movements but in building his chest and upper-body strength.

Looker then moves to the heart of his biographical project. He claims to have challenged Roosevelt to submit himself to his, Looker's, lengthy observation and later to a medical examination by prominent physicians. Roosevelt took the challenge and invited Looker to spend time in the governor's mansion and to observe him for several days as he went through his daily routines. This arrangement was made, claims Looker, with no political underhandedness. Thus, Looker reports that Roosevelt was frank about his infantile paralysis experience and what, if any, limitations it placed on him.

But for greater objectivity, Looker writes that he wanted to hear about Roosevelt's health from others as well. Roosevelt, declares Looker, easily agreed to this challenge. "I want," Looker states, "the real evidence which was created before there was the slightest possibility of its having political implication. I want to see your own personal letter files of the time. There must be correspondence there that will give me the opportunity to dig the facts out—independently."[20] Roosevelt, Looker reports, was very willing to give him any evidence requested. Thus, Looker was given permission to review all of Roosevelt's personal files from 1924 to 1926 with no selection and without any record being removed. What, then, was Roosevelt hiding from 1921 to 1923?

Looker documents a letter Roosevelt wrote to Warm Springs owner George Foster Peabody on October 14, 1924, which states that "nothing finer nor more useful to humanity could be done than to establish a 'cure' where the best of treatment along the lines of the accepted treatment could be given." In 1931–32, however, Roosevelt considered the word "cure" to be "misleading," telling Looker that he had used it in the letter in the sense of "place for treatment." More important to Roosevelt now, claimed Looker, was to "avoid the word [cure] as far as possible," in order "not to spread the false impression that there are miraculous medicinal qualities in the pool or a guarantee of cure in the treatment."[21]

Looker documents a syndicated newspaper story that described Roosevelt as "Swimming Back to Health" and told of him swimming with Annette Kellerman, a famous swimmer who also was afflicted with infantile paralysis earlier in her life. In those early days, Roosevelt, motivated by his own plan for recovery, pushed others to find solutions, cures, and exercises to help polio victims. This motivation was manifested in Roosevelt's enthusiasm for investing in the dilapidated Warm Springs resort, his push to have the American Orthopedic Association recognize the value of underwater treatment, and his own efforts to help other polio victims without any particular scientific or professional background. Roosevelt's convictions regarding the treatment of polio resulted in his investment in Warm Springs and the official agreement in 1926 to buy the property from Peabody and turn it into a polio treatment center.

In his first campaign since contracting polio, his first run at the governorship of New York, Roosevelt faced the health issue head on, claims Looker. He was referred to as "that man on crutches they [Smith and his people] have put up for Governor!" Roosevelt won by more than twenty-five thousand votes, and some apparently voted for him out of sympathy. To strengthen his book's argument that Roosevelt was fit to be president, Looker points to Wilson and Harding, who "cracked physically under the strain of the Presidency. As a nation we have come to accept as an axiom that a sound mind in a sound body is demanded for the Presidency."[22]

Looker documents in his book the letter he sent Roosevelt on February 23, 1931, in which he writes that "even though you have recovered from your attack of infantile paralysis, the strain of the Presidency will be such as to seriously raise the question as to whether or not you are physically fit to be President. . . . I am writing to ask that you make a frank avowal as to whether or not, in the event of your nomination, you are sufficiently recovered to assure your supporters that you could stand the strain of the Presidency."[23]

Roosevelt replied on February 28, 1931,

> Of course no statement from me as to my physical fitness should really be acceptable to you. Your question, however, is very distinctly a personal challenge to me, no matter what my present or future position as a public servant may be—even in the humblest of positions. Furthermore, not being in any sense a candidate for any other public office, it is equally a challenge to any business or professional work which I may assume on leaving Albany. Being assured of your integrity, I am therefore prepared to permit you to make an investigation of my physical fitness, to give you every facility for thoroughly making it, and authority for you to publish its results without censorship from me.[24]

To add credibility to the seemingly innocent arrangement, Looker writes that "the challenge had been caught and thrown back within four days. My letter to him had been almost brutal in tone. It had in no way expressed a personally sincere anxiety to see fair play. I had shown I belonged to the opposition."[25]

Looker goes on and plants questions that "clearly" indicate how fit Roosevelt is. In his book, Looker reports writing to Roosevelt, "But Governor, I am not questioning your mental fitness as a result of infantile paralysis, because I understand that the disease is not connected with the brain." "You're quite right," answered Roosevelt, "but the fact is not generally understood, and in fairness to myself as well as to all others who have been touched by it, you must not only make this clear but use my own case as proof."[26] The question and answer notwithstanding, the naiveté here is striking.

Roosevelt used the book *This Man Roosevelt* to express his reluctance to run for the presidency despite his personal ambition: "Was I personally anxious to be Governor? I was not! But I accepted that nomination in order to accept an opportunity for service. You [Looker] must understand I have to use the old words, and that one particularly—service—because no other word exactly fits. I feel the same way about the Presidency." For additional support, Looker quotes Eleanor's reply to the question about her husband's fitness: "'If the infantile paralysis didn't kill him, the Presidency won't.'"[27]

Looker made several observations regarding Roosevelt's health and passed them on as if they were made by an expert: "His [Roosevelt's] walk is slow but steady and in no sense halting. His legs, being locked in their braces, swing forward like a pendulum set in motion from the hips. The moment his foot is firmly planted he swings his other foot forward. The only reason for his braces is to insure [*sic*] his knees locking. This is necessarily awkward but it does not result in fatigue." Looker continued, "The best demonstration of how the braces work was given by the Governor's son, James. He put the braces on himself. He found he could walk easily, once he had mastered the motion. But, despite the fact that he was an athlete . . . , he could not climb stairs with them but collapsed again and again while his father shouted with laughter."[28] From all other accounts, Roosevelt could not walk without assistance, the use of braces was difficult, and his walk was very slow. Looker significantly minimizes the role of the leg braces, however, and the father laughing at his son's inability to walk with the braces implies that Franklin Roosevelt had no such difficulties with his mobility.

Looker describes the agreement among press correspondents and photographers to refrain from comment on Roosevelt's disability, and he indicates that photographers later destroyed existing photographs that clearly showed his disability. Looker commented, "The behavior of the news and the camera men is real tribute to Roosevelt's personality. But even a gentleman's conspiracy of silence at this moment is hardly fair to Roosevelt. Mystery with regard to his condition would breed all sorts of unfounded rumors."[29] Looker, being Roosevelt's mouthpiece, puts forward two objectives: to encourage the press to respect Roosevelt's disability and treat it as a private matter and not a public one and to encourage the press to report accurately on Roosevelt's physical fitness—as long as such accuracy was in line with Looker's description.

Looker writes that he had "walked with him [Roosevelt] many times from the entrance hall into the Capitol, some fifty paces, to the elevator running up to the Executive Chamber. Walking some twenty paces more from the desk, he eases himself into his big Governor's chair and flexes his leg braces so that his knees bend under the edge of his desk. He seems unfatigued." Frances Perkins's account is more credible. She describes how painful it was to watch Roosevelt being carried into a room and how slow and arduous it was for Roosevelt get himself seated.[30]

Looker, loyal to his mission to prove Roosevelt's fitness, supplied further proof of his subject's fitness. He noted that "it is worth recording, since all the details are essential if his physical condition is discussed, that he has not lost any feeling in any part of his legs or feet." For proof, Looker recounts hearing the governor being highly amused one day, saying, "The soles of my feet are so ticklish that I was having a terrible time getting my socks on!"[31] In other words, Roosevelt could feel his feet, and that meant that his recovery had continued successfully.

The committee of specialists Looker organized as part of his supposedly public "challenge" to Roosevelt was selected by Dr. Linsly R. Williams, director of the New York Academy of Medicine. The specialists were Dr. Samuel W. Lambert (physician), Dr. Russell A. Hibbs (orthopedist), and Dr. Foster Kennedy (neurologist). The medical examination took place on April 29, 1931, in Roosevelt's Manhattan residence. Looker was present in the house but did not witness the actual examination.

Two reports were issued thereafter. The first report was short and testified that Roosevelt's "health and powers of endurance are such as to allow him to meet any demand of private and public life." A longer report, also dated April 29, 1931, attested to Roosevelt's healthy organs and functions, his normal spinal column, its perfect alignment, and the freedom from disease. The report concluded that "there has been progressive recovery of power in the legs" since Roosevelt contracted polio in 1921, and that "this restoration continues and will continue." The final statement was most assuring: "Governor Roosevelt can walk all necessary distances and can maintain a standing position without fatigue." Looker added his own observation: "Roosevelt's improvement has been distinctly discernible even in the period of my observation." Finally, Looker stated the conclusion that his book project had been designed to produce: "Infantile paralysis is no detriment to Franklin Roosevelt. He is physically fit to be President."[32] Thus had the provocative, perhaps sensational, *Liberty Magazine* query been answered.

On November 17, 1932, Roosevelt sent Looker a letter; in it he wrote, "Things have moved fast in this week since November eighth and it has become perfectly clear to me that future articles—at least for a long time—are taboo. . . . The situation during the pre-convention year was, of course, entirely different as it was during the campaign itself."[33] This letter is the only one in which Roosevelt came close to indicating his arrangement with Looker. Most of the details of such a stunt were revealed by Looker in his correspondence with Roosevelt. Now, Roosevelt asked Looker to stop the arrangement. He no longer needed Looker's help in "proving" his fitness. He was now president-elect.

Looker surfaced again, though, as he wrote the president on November 13, 1933. He was probably unhappy that the *New York Herald Tribune,* in reviewing his book on Roosevelt, called him "'wholly loyal to the President'" and an admirer of the president, implying the book's bias. Even the *New York Times Book Review,* Looker wrote Roosevelt, referred to him as an "'apologist when the need arises, and he writes with a degree of animation . . . that may occasionally carry him beyond the limits of evidence.'" "Other comments," continued Looker, "I don't quote; I suffer so much under them," he wrote, adding that "I get it in the neck for being loyal to you, and I'll probably get in it the neck for my criticism. Hah! That is not a laugh."[34] Roosevelt replied on November 21, 1933: "Dear Earle: 'Hah! Hah!' and again 'Hah!' said the duck laughing. However, being a practical business man, I suggest stirring up Foreign controversy over your opus. This will sell a million copies. Yours in misery."[35] The ingratiating Looker was hoping for some reward for his loyalty, but alas, Roosevelt had the last laugh.

Earle Looker has since become a very small footnote in Roosevelt scholarship. Clearly he was an obsequious man looking to gain privilege from his relationship with the powerful and famous. That Roosevelt largely cut him off following the publication and success of the *Liberty Magazine* article, however, should not predispose us to see him as a small, insignificant player in Roosevelt's quest for the presidency. Whether we would deem the article and the activity around it a "stunt" or all "cooked up," Earle Looker had accomplished something that no one in the Roosevelt inner circle had even attempted: an article in a mass circulation outlet that testified credibly to the soon-to-be candidate's physical abilities to do the job of president. Previously, Roosevelt had relied on the press to report fairly and accurately on his health. As the presidential campaign neared, though, his patience with the press had clearly worn thin. So, in 1931, he did the only "logical" thing: He infiltrated the media by proxy to deliver his own message with a veneer of objectivity.

6 A New Deal and a New Body

THE POLITICAL MACHINATIONS BETWEEN EARLE LOOKER and Franklin Roosevelt were doubtless successful; many of *Liberty Magazine's* readers were likely convinced that Roosevelt was a healthy, vigorous man with nothing to hide about his disability. But not all were. As the primary season drew near, the whispering campaign again kicked into high gear. The whispering, of course, was tied directly to Roosevelt's presidential aspirations. As *Time* reported, "One sure evidence of Governor Roosevelt's lead toward the nomination was the recent spread of unfavorable stories about his health."[1]

Drawing largely on his experiences from the 1928 gubernatorial race, Roosevelt did not take the whispering campaign lying down. Instead, as we document in this chapter and the next, he opted for the one method over which he had direct control: showing his body to the nation's electorate. If Jim Farley could not quell the whispering interpersonally, if Earle Looker could not stop it in one of the nation's largest circulation magazines, and if Louis Howe could not put a halt to the rumors and innuendo through his voluminous correspondence, Roosevelt, as was often the case, would take the issue directly to the people, thereby effectively asking them to make a judgment about his fitness for office. With seven years and more of careful preparation, he no doubt felt confident of his body, of what it could not do and what it could. He also had four years of carefully scripted deception behind him in Albany.

But Roosevelt's problems as 1932 dawned were not strictly physical. He also had rhetorical problems: Howe, Col. Edward M. House, and Samuel I. Rosenman were simply not writing very good speeches for the candidate. As was his penchant, Roosevelt went to the universities for help, in this case seeking out a Columbia University political scientist by the name of Raymond Moley. Moley, an Olmsted Falls, Ohio, native, would prove to be a terrific rhetorician, as Roosevelt's first Inaugural Address, among other writings, would attest.

Moley had no doubt heard the whispering about Roosevelt's health. Perhaps he had initially been inclined to believe some of it, as a letter to his sister Nell suggests. He wrote, "The stories about his illness and its effect upon him are the bunk. Nobody in public life since T. R. [Theodore Roosevelt] has been so robust, so buoyantly and blatantly healthful as this fellow. He is full of animal spirits. . . . The man's energy and vitality are astounding."[2] Moley's face-to-face meeting with the governor had revealed the whispering to be "bunk"; it was a lesson in perception, in embodied conversation, that he would not forget during the campaign.

Moley's optimistic note to his sister was without question influenced by the intoxicating elixir he had experienced in the aftermath of Roosevelt's first national campaign speech, delivered on April 7: the generally well-received "forgotten man" oration. It was Moley's first major rhetorical effort in what would prove to be a highly successful partnership. Roosevelt began the speech by reminding his listeners that fifteen years earlier, he had answered the call to public duty during World War I and that the "whole Nation mobilized for war, economic, industrial, social, and military resources gathered into a vast unit . . . the scales of ten million men equipped with physical needs and sustained by the realization that behind them were the united efforts of 110,000,000 human beings." "In my calm judgment," announced Roosevelt, "the Nation faces today a more grave emergency than in 1917."[3] The call was clear. The great mobilization of World War I was now needed to combat the Great Depression. Roosevelt, like his idol Wilson before him, would lead this impressive mobilization.

The grounding of the call to action lay in the symbolic figure of the forgotten man. "These unhappy times," continued Roosevelt, "call for the building of plans that rest upon the forgotten, the unorganized but the indispensable units of economic power, for plans like those of 1917 that build from bottom up . . . put their faith once more in the forgotten man at the bottom of the economic pyramid."[4] Unlike Napoleon, who "lost the battle of Waterloo because he forgot his infantry," Roosevelt positioned himself as the responsible head of a people's army, the champion of average citizens, who were the real sufferers of the depression.[5]

Roosevelt proposed a pragmatic solution against what he called the more shallow ones. Even if billions of dollars were raised for useful public works, he argued, those projects could not supply work to the seven million to ten million unemployed: "Let us admit frankly that it would be only a stop-gap. A real economic cure must go to the killing of the bacteria in the system rather then to the treatment of external symptoms." The mixing of war and military metaphors with medical ones is not surprising. "Dr. Roosevelt" would go the root of the problem to eradicate its effects once and for all instead of treating only its symptoms. To achieve all of that, Roosevelt concluded with a call to courage in handling the current emergency that was "equal to that of war. Let us mobilize to meet it."[6] The immobile presidential nominee would do his best rhetorically to mobilize the nation.

Western and southern states appreciated the speech, but it was vague, and journalist Walter Lippmann chastised Roosevelt for not giving details as to how he would achieve the increase in purchasing power. Even the erstwhile presidential contender, Al Smith, joined the attack on Roosevelt. Indeed, the call for mobilizing the nation and the need to kill the bacteria came with no clear indications of what specific policy measures Roosevelt had in mind. Regardless, the popular reaction, which counted the most, was very favorable. Roosevelt found the fitting appeal to reach the "forgotten man."

Roosevelt's presidential ambitions brought to the surface a growing tension with Al Smith. While he was able to maintain cordial relations with Smith upon becoming governor, by the time he was reelected in 1930 in the midst of the depression, the Smith camp had begun to realize the seriousness of the Roosevelt candidacy. The result was the beginning of a "Stop Roosevelt" movement. In January, 1932, with the primaries under way, the tension between Roosevelt and Smith intensified, though both maintained the appearance of cordiality. Roosevelt had now two opponents to contend with: the Republican administration and other Democratic contenders. Each perceived the health issue as a factor to manipulate, though Democratic opposition was by and large careful and cautious in exploiting Roosevelt's disability.

Just eleven days after his "forgotten man" speech, Roosevelt delivered his Jefferson Day speech in Saint Paul, Minnesota. The address would become known as the "Concert of Interests" speech, but Roosevelt did not deliver it as initially drafted by Moley's colleague at Columbia, Rexford G. Tugwell, and refined by himself and Moley. The version that he eventually delivered was, in Tugwell's words, "terrible."[7] Tugwell's judgment stemmed from Roosevelt's lengthy digression on public utilities regulation—a digression that comprised nearly 40 percent of the entire speech. Just as he had focused on George Washington's extensive travel in an earlier speech, Roosevelt tied, ever so loosely, his theme of "universality of interest" with Thomas Jefferson's method of governing by travel. "I can picture the weeks on horseback," he said, "when he [Jefferson] was traveling into the different States of the Union, slowly and laboriously accumulating an understanding of the people of his country."[8] Roosevelt, who advocated a traveling campaign against the advice of his aides, found support for this political method in the practices of the Founding Fathers. He also implied that his travel made him more knowledgeable than his opponent and brought him closer to the nation's problems.

The knowledge and experience he gained allowed Roosevelt to diagnose the situation. Indeed, the economic situation was grave, he announced, stating "that a great fear has swept the country few can doubt. Normal times lull us into complacency. We become lazy and contented. Then with the coming of economic stress we feel the disturbing hand of fear." Fear would become Roosevelt's main weapon in his rhetorical arsenal. He gained much from this strategy by alluding to his courage, both personal and political. "This fear," he continued, "spreads to the entire country and with more or less unity we turn to our common Government at Washington. In meeting this appeal, what has the present Republican administration done and what is the policy and spirit that has guided it?"[9]

While the Hoover administration answered the call to alleviate fear with the "panic-stricken policy of delay and improvisation," Roosevelt's solution, mindful of the criticism he received for suggesting a planned economy, was a modification of his earlier position. He explained that he did not envision a completely planned and regimented economy but rather the need for "a community of interest": "I am not speaking of an economic life completely planned and regimented. I am speaking of the necessity, however, in those imperative interferences with the economic life of the Nation that there be a real community of interest, not only among the sections of this great country, but among its economic units and the various groups in these units; that there be common participation in the work of remedial figures, planned on the basis of a shared common life, the low as well as the high."[10]

And the rationale for this approach? "In much of our present plans there is too much disposition to mistake the part for the whole, the head for the body, the captain for the company, the general for the army. I plead not for a class control but for a true concert of interests." Roosevelt explained his concert of interests philosophy with the help of military and body metaphors. The metaphors collectively presented Roosevelt as the head, the captain, and the general. The mobility-conscious Roosevelt concluded his address with an appeal to many not to heed the call of the opposition "'not to swap horses crossing a stream,'" not to "'swap toboggans while you are sliding downhill.'" The more accurate plea, stated Roosevelt, should be: "'If the old car in spite of frequent emergency repairs has been bumping along downhill on only two cylinders for three long years, it is time to get another car that will start uphill on all four.'" Roosevelt, of course, took the more difficult task of moving uphill in addition to replacing an undrivable and hardly mobile administration. He also went with the more expensive option of replacing a car in the midst of a depression. Was this a note of confidence? Quoting from Lincoln, Roosevelt called on the nation to "go forward without fear and with manly hearts." The speech concluded as it began, with a call for the courage to move the nation without the constraints of fear.[11]

Quietly, away from the vicissitudes of the campaign trail, Herbert Hoover was rooting against the Stop Roosevelt forces; he desperately wanted his old friend from the Wilson administration to come out of Chicago with his party's nomination. Part of Hoover's desire for a Roosevelt candidacy stemmed from his view of the candidate's mental (in)abilities; to the president, Roosevelt was a lightweight, no match for the brilliant mining engineer turned philanthropist, turned shrewd negotiator, turned innovative commerce secretary. But Hoover was also aware of Roosevelt's disability, as were those immediately around him in the White House. And, not surprisingly, Roosevelt's disability was a potentially consequential electoral liability. Theodore Joslin, Hoover's press secretary, noted as much in a diary entry in February, 1932: "1932 is not 1928. I would prefer Roosevelt to almost any of the leading Democrat[s] for the President's opponent for the people would come to understand he has not the ability nor the mentality to be President." Joslin elaborated further on the issue of "ability": "He is a paralytic, depriving him of the physical strength proper to handle the duties of President."[12] Al Smith had made a similar mistake just a few years earlier, figuring Roosevelt for a disabled governor who would gladly turn over the legislative reigns to Smith and his minions ensconced at Albany.

Others in the Hoover administration saw Roosevelt's disability as an index of his imperiled masculinity. James H. MacLafferty, a former congressman from California and Hoover's mole on Capitol Hill during his presidency, figured Roosevelt's disability along gendered lines. In a diary entry of January 15, 1932, he described Roosevelt's speech from the day before "as a very lady-like affair." To Hoover, he continued, "'Well, the democrats had their say again last night. I am afraid that if Frank Roosevelt is your opponent the campaign will be too ladylike.'"[13] The rough-and-tumble world of presidential electoral politics was a male space, a masculine space, not a place for "ladies" like Roosevelt. That Roosevelt's lady-like ways were linked to his disability is suggested in MacLafferty's diary entry of April 21: "Frank Roosevelt will likely be Hoover's opponent and God knows the country is beginning to laugh at his pussy-footing. He is a pussy-footer and in politics he has always been one."[14]

Less than a week later, the events of April 27, 1932, would prove momentous for reasons also related to disability and public appearances. The nation's governors were nearby in Virginia for their annual conference, and Hoover had invited them to dine with him at the White House. The Roosevelts, as was their custom in dealing with Franklin's disability, arrived early. Hoover arrived late—about half an hour so. During this time Franklin stood, for fear that if he sat, the whispering would begin anew among the assembled governors. And so he stood, perspiring profusely from the unusually hot and muggy weather. Franklin and Eleanor were furious, certain that the delay was purposeful on Hoover's part. That evening, after the dinner, Joslin recorded his (and Hoover's) impressions: "Back in the office tonight, we discussed the elections in Mass[achusetts] and Pennsylvania, with the President strongly of the opinion the results mean the elimination of Roosevelt. He shouldn't think of running. He is a sick man. He wouldn't live a year in the White House."[15]

But the president did not have the last laugh regarding the events of April 27. Physical appearances also concerned the president and his wife. On April 30 Joslin recorded in his diary, "He was wild about the movietones taken of him at the [G]overnor's Conference. 'They were horrible,' he told me after seeing them last night. 'My worst fears were realized. They make me look as though I was 82 years old.'" But Hoover, like Roosevelt, had more partisan and electoral matters on the mind: "'Worst of all, posed pictures of Roosevelt and [Maryland governor Albert C.] Ritchie were woven into them. They looked young and vigorous. I was made to appear aged and decrepid [sic]. They were entirely misrepresented to you. That is the end of indoor movietones. Mrs. Hoover was so disturbed that she broke down and cried.'"[16]

As April ended, things were not so good in the Roosevelt camp either. Several months earlier Jim Farley had predicted a first ballot victory in Chicago; by late April and early May, Howe "shuddered" at the "distinct possibility that his beloved Franklin would not be nominated at all!"[17] On April 26, Roosevelt was trounced badly in Massachusetts by Smith. On May 2, Connecticut pledged its delegates to Smith. Rhode Island and New Jersey followed suit two weeks later. And the coveted California delegation pledged its votes to the powerful William Randolph Hearst's candidate of choice, the Speaker of the House from Texas, John Nance Garner.

Despite these setbacks, a Roosevelt victory was still in sight, as Jim Farley details. Recall that Earle Looker had earlier advised Roosevelt "to create something of dramatic importance which will provide grand copy before the convention." Nearly a year later, Farley and Roosevelt, no doubt along with Howe and Moley, had crystallized plans for what that "something" would be. "Early that evening [April 23, 1932] I talked with Governor Roosevelt in his New York home," Farley began. "He indicated he might change his plans about going to Chicago. His first plan was to wire the members of the National Committee to remain in Chicago until he got there. . . . He could address the Committee and make definite plans to get down to work." Farley was in agreement with such plans, but he urged Roosevelt to consider something far more dramatic: "I felt it would be a good idea if he could make plans to get to Chicago before the Convention adjourned and address the entire assemblage."[18] What remained to be planned was exactly how Roosevelt would "get to" Chicago to make such an address.

The nation, if it was reading carefully, received an intimation on May 16, 1932, that Roosevelt might attempt something dramatic. The *New York Times* reported "that a whispering campaign about his physical condition was being spread throughout the Middle West in an effort to head off his nomination by the Democrats in Chicago." Furthermore, Ike Dunlap, a friend then visiting Roosevelt at Warm Springs, reportedly "suggested that it might be well for the Executive to enter into some activity which could be broadcast to demonstrate his physical fitness."[19] That broadcast, we argue, involved both Roosevelt's flight to Chicago and his acceptance speech.

Several weeks prior to the convention, Roosevelt secretly chartered a Ford Trimotor airplane. Should he win the party's nomination, he would fly to Chicago and receive it in person. Such an embodied acceptance was not part of party tradition. Prior to 1932, the winning candidate would only be "informed" of the nomination several weeks after the convention had concluded. He would then make an obligatory acceptance speech—usually to a small crowd of delegates. In making his travel plans, Roosevelt had several options: He could drive to the convention; he could proceed to Chicago by train; and he even kidded that he might rent a five-seat bicycle so that his sons could peddle him there.[20] Instead, he selected the most dramatic form of transportation.

Chronologically far removed from the exigencies of Roosevelt's health, contemporary commentators such as Stephen Skowronek claim that the principal significance of the flight to the Democratic National Convention was its stunning repudiation of tradition—a gesture that presages, and would be the hallmark of, the Roosevelt administration. "This stunning display of independence by a nominee," Skowronek argues, "crystallized in an instant a profound change in traditional relationships between candidates and the organizations they were chosen to represent."[21]

Those a bit closer in time to the scene, while they still recognized the flight as a rhetorically charged move, offer a very different interpretation. The *Chicago Tribune* opined that "utilization of the plane for a quick jump, it is hoped, will offset any propaganda that the governor is physically unfit to meet the duties of the presidency."[22] Similarly, albeit tending toward the hagiographic, Arthur Sears Henning declared that "the man who has all but recovered from the paralysis of the legs with which he was stricken a decade ago had come to show the people that he is not physically disqualified for the exacting duties of the presidency."[23] Authors Roy V. Peel and Thomas C. Donnelly note, "The quick jump across the country also helped greatly to dispel any belief that the governor was physically weak or that he was not a man of action."[24]

Each "reading" of the flight was confirmed nearly forty years later by an insider's account. Roosevelt's son Elliott, who frequently walked by his father's side, states that his father "wanted to demonstrate by this gesture that he was a man of vigorous action, not the semi-invalid depicted without fail by his enemies in both parties."[25] The "gesture," we should not forget, was also an act of no small bravery; aviation was still very much in its infancy. As author Lela Stiles summarizes, "The idea was to prove once and for all that Franklin Roosevelt was a normal man in spite of the inactivity of his legs."[26]

But before such drama would unfold, Roosevelt delivered his final, pre-convention campaign speech at Oglethorpe University on May 22. The speech has a rather bizarre genesis. At a mid-May picnic in Warm Springs, Roosevelt biographer and *New York Herald Tribune* reporter Ernest K. Lindley, among others, ribbed the governor for his noncommittal speeches. Roosevelt reportedly challenged, "'If you fellows think my speeches are so bad, why don't you write one for me?'"[27] Two days later Lindley handed him one, and he used the draft "practically verbatim."[28] Not surprisingly, it bore little resemblance to Roosevelt's earlier speeches, particularly his Jefferson Day address.

Much had indeed changed from Roosevelt's 1926 "Quo Vadis?" commencement address, which was a somber account of a chaotic future the graduating class would meet. In the Lindley-drafted speech at Oglethorpe University, Roosevelt stated that waste, lack of foresight, and a multitude of views as to how to revive the economy were some of the problematic factors. He suggested that Hoover viewed the depression as a natural phenomenon in a natural economic cycle. "According to this theory," stated Roosevelt, "if we grin and bear long enough, the economic machine will eventually begin to pick up speed and in the course of an indefinite number of years will again attain that maximum number of revolutions which signifies what we have been wont to miscall prosperity, but which, alas, is but a last ostentatious twirl of the economic machine before it again succumbs to that mysterious impulse to slow down again."[29] This speech was not Roosevelt's, and the metaphorical shift is evident. The economy was now an engine, a less common metaphor than the body and motion metaphors Roosevelt might have employed.

The message, however, remained intact. Roosevelt believed that organizations could influence economic behavior, unlike those who considered a nation's economy to be a natural process that should not be tampered with. In light of this view, Roosevelt could talk about the need "to inject life into our ailing economic order." The medical metaphor appeared in one short paragraph. Practically, the injection of life meant the need to "bring about a wiser, more equitable distribution of the national income." Thus, "The country needs and, unless I mistake its temper, the country demands bold, persistent experimentation." This bold approach required "enthusiasm, imagination and the ability to face facts, even unpleasant ones, bravely."[30] Uncle Fred Delano could not have said it better himself.

With the Democratic National Convention under way by late June, Hoover, Joslin, and MacLafferty spectated anxiously. On June 28, 1932, Hoover asked his press secretary whether he thought Roosevelt would be nominated. "'Absolutely,' I replied. 'He'll get it on the second or third ballot.' 'I hope so,' the President continued. 'Our salvation lies largely in his nomination. . . . 'I am afraid of [Newton] Baker,' the President said."[31] On July 1, after three ballots, William Gibbs McAdoo, the same man who expressed shock at the severity of his friend's illness eleven years earlier, released California's delegates to Roosevelt, and thus began the fourth-ballot victory for Franklin Roosevelt. Back at the White House, Joslin recorded just how pleased Hoover was with the outcome. "Usher carried news of R's nomination to Hoover. He telephoned back that the President smiled more broadly than he had in months when he received the message."[32]

With the nomination now secure, Roosevelt put his team's plan into action. Roosevelt could feign obsequiousness when he needed to, and so with pencil and paper he wrote to the Chicago delegates from New York: "May I suggest if the convention concurs that I come to Chicago at once for the purpose of meeting and greeting the Delegates and alternatives before they return to their homes." Roosevelt was not forthcoming about the plan to show himself to the nation as well as the delegates: "In these times it is easier and less expensive for one man to journey to a great party gathering now meeting than to ask many to come from every state to Albany at a future date."[33] Of course, the delegates were not going to refuse such an offer, and so with several members of his family, the Democratic presidential candidate set out for Chicago early on July 2.

James MacLafferty was incredulous when he learned of the risky and visible scheme. He recorded that he and Hoover spoke "of the fact that Roosevelt was to fly to the convention today and that he would address that body. I said that the audience would see Roosevelt's physical helplessness and that I marveled at their willingness to put a man as physically incapacitated as he at the head of government." Hoover was one step ahead of MacLafferty, however. "Mr. Hoover said that the audience would not be allowed to see Roosevelt's helplessness but that it would be cleverly concealed by the skillful handling of him." Hoover was attuned to such handling because "he had noticed this when Roosevelt was recently at the White House to attend the dinner he, Hoover, had given to the governors of many states [on April 27]. He said that newspaper cameramen had attempted to get pictures of Roosevelt as he was being helped out of his automobile but they were prevented by Roosevelt's military aides who kept so close as to prevent it." Nonetheless, MacLafferty insisted that the plan was poorly designed: "I said that I knew the locale of everything in the convention hall at Chicago and that the audience would have to see his helplessness when he took the platform to address them." Hoover knew that Roosevelt had thought through the logistics: "Mr. Hoover still insisted that in spite of that it would be concealed." MacLafferty closed his diary entry facetiously. Little could he have guessed that such plans would come to fruition in just a few months: "Roosevelt and Garner should tour the country in the campaign together because in fairness to the country the people should be made to realize Roosevelt's terrible physical affliction and also that they might see just how funny Garner looks."[34]

Meanwhile, the expectations and drama created by Roosevelt's eight-hour flight seemed to necessitate an equally stirring acceptance speech, especially given that it would be broadcast live to the nation. The importance of the speech, especially its masterful yet subtle emphasis on Roosevelt's health, Hoover's sickness, and the nation's impending recovery, is underscored in a book by one of its chief architects, Raymond Moley. In painstaking detail, Moley recounts the events leading up to the speech, including the shocking revelation that the speech was almost not delivered.[35] For several weeks prior to the convention, Moley, Roosevelt, and Samuel Rosenman had worked on the speech—an association that worried and angered Howe.

Howe was always protective of "the boss," but he was particularly incensed by Rosenman's rhetorical influence. Howe was suspicious that Rosenman's hand would be clearly visible in the speech, a suspicion that was confirmed when he had the entire speech read to him over the telephone immediately following Roosevelt's nomination. Despite a very high fever and fatigue from not sleeping at the convention, Howe immediately set to writing another acceptance speech. The following day, Moley's worst-case scenario had become a reality: Howe greeted Roosevelt at the airport with a new speech. As the motorcade headed toward the Congress Hotel, Roosevelt alternately waved to the sweltering masses and glanced at Howe's draft. Somewhere during the ride, he reached a decision. Roosevelt "walked" into the boisterous convention hall with his lower half carefully hidden from view as Hoover had predicted. As he mounted the platform, Moley, from the back of the convention hall, strained to hear the words with which he had grown familiar. To his dismay, he did not hear them. But, just a few paragraphs into the speech, the familiarity returned. Roosevelt had simply substituted Howe's first page for the first page of the earlier draft.

The five-paragraph exordium was the stuff of standard political fare:

Roosevelt thanked his audience, he praised previous party leaders, and he expressed his commitment to the party. At closer inspection, though, Roosevelt called attention to the physical body—his own, his listeners', and the deceased body of Woodrow Wilson. In fact, the very first sentence emphasized a corporate corporeality and the physical demands endured by both speaker and listener: "I appreciate your willingness after these six arduous days to remain here, for I know well the sleepless hours which you and I have had." The fact that Roosevelt experienced the arduousness of six days and still insisted on flying to the convention underscored his physical stamina. Additionally, Roosevelt's late arrival—a subtle but important disclaimer related to his physical presence in Chicago—had nothing to do with his health but instead related to the unpredictable "winds of Heaven." The winds were so strong and posed such a physical threat that Roosevelt "could only be thankful for my Navy training."[36] His reference to the navy is intriguing, for it suggests a military presence and military leadership— images that belie any sense of sickness or enervation. By calling attention to his naval training, despite it being two decades removed, Roosevelt thus subsumed his postpolio body within his World War I–era body.

He called further attention to his physical appearance and, by implication, his physical health, by elaborating on the symbolic meaning of his flight. The flight, he claimed, was "symbolic" of his intention to break "foolish traditions" and to "avoid all hypocrisy or sham." His "unprecedented and unusual" flight was warranted by the "unprecedented and unusual times"—what Kenneth Burke would term a "scenic" imperative. That the scene may have more strictly biological motivations is underscored by the corresponding imagery that Roosevelt utilized. The flight represented his unwillingness "to avoid all silly shutting of the eyes to the truth in this campaign. You have nominated me and I know it, and I am here to thank you for the honor."[37] Roosevelt, of course, could have easily acknowledged his nomination via radio, but such a disembodied gesture would not have focused the delegates' (and the nation's) collective gaze on their candidate. Roosevelt's ocular reference not only implied his willingness to be seen, it also linked truth and reality with an ability to see clearly—a linkage, and its opposite (blindness), that recur throughout the speech.

Roosevelt then made a transition from the visual to the peripatetic, and therein did he first provide verbal testimony to his ability to walk and, by inheritance from President Wilson, to lead: "Let us now and here highly resolve to resume the country's *uninterrupted march along the path* of real progress. . . . Our indomitable leader in that *interrupted march* is no longer with us, but there still survives today his spirit. Many of his captains, thank God, are still with us, to give us wise counsel. Let us *feel* that in everything we do there still lives with us, *if not the body,* the great indomitable, un-quenchable, progressive soul of our Commander-in-Chief, Woodrow Wil-son" (emphasis added).[38]

To march is not simply to walk; it is to walk with purpose, discipline, and direction. And Roosevelt, as former assistant secretary of the navy under Wilson, was a qualified captain, a leader who could take over where Wilson had left off. That Roosevelt was *the* captain to lead the Wilson army is at-tested to by the spatio-temporal marker "now and here," a marker that not only called attention, again, to the symbolic importance of the flight but also highlighted Roosevelt's legitimacy as a fitting heir to the body and soul of Woodrow Wilson. This latter point was certainly at issue as the conven-tion unfolded: Wilson's former secretary of war, Newton Baker, was ru-mored to be the dark-horse candidate should Roosevelt's pledged delegates prove tractable. In fact, prior to the fourth and deciding ballot, Roosevelt telephoned Baker and promised him the nomination should he want it. Baker politely declined. Thus did Roosevelt inherit, perhaps by default, Wilson's bodily and ideological legacy.

Having justified his physical abilities to lead the Wilson army and "en-ter this new battle," Roosevelt moved to discuss the opposing views of the "Republican leaders" and the Democratic party with respect to the nation's "economic and social life." But, before juxtaposing those who support "blind reaction on the one *hand*" and "the party with clean *hands,*" he of-fered a very physical warning to members of both parties: "Here and now I invite those nominal Republicans who *find* that their *conscience* cannot be squared with the *groping* and the failure of their party leaders to *join hands* with us; here and now, in equal measure, I warn those nominal Democrats who *squint* at the future with their *faces* turned toward the past, and who *feel* no responsibility to the demands of the new time, that they are *out of step* with their Party" (emphasis added).[39] Not only did Roosevelt again uti-lize the spatio-temporal marker to underscore the flight and his physical presence, but he turned the tables on his conservative brethren. Smith, Raskob, and Jouett Shouse, the conservative triumvirate, were the "real" cripples for not being able to keep up with the party's progressive move-ment under the leadership of its marching nominee. Roosevelt employed the imagery of hands and feet to suggest a corporeal fusion of feeling—a physical solidarity, not an unwelcome sexuality, was offered. Hoover and other Republican party leaders were guilty of unspecified sins against the body politic. That they were sins of and against the body is emphasized by the appeal to hands "groping" in the dark—a bodily invasion that has its moral expression "squarely" in the conscience.

The moral repugnance, though, pales in comparison to the sort of Frankenstein economic monster birthed by Hoover and his cohorts. For

Roosevelt the nation's economy was an embodied and observable phenomenon, expressed in terms of "the clear fact of our economic condition." This condition had been adversely affected by the Republicans' deformed progeny: "The people will not forget the claim made by them [Republican leaders] then [1928] that prosperity was only a domestic product *manufactured* by a Republican President and a Republican Congress. If they claim *paternity* for the one they cannot deny *paternity* for the other" (emphasis added).[40] The metaphors, at first glance, seem badly mixed; birthing and building seem to entail very different sorts of correspondences. Furthermore, how could a Republican president (male) and a Republican Congress (male) give birth to offspring?

The divergent metaphors are perhaps explicable within the context of the Hoover presidency. Hoover, we should remember, was elected as "The Great Engineer," someone who could apply the rationalism and precision associated with engineering to the nation's social and economic issues. Hoover was seen by many as cold and calculating, a person who could literally "build" economic progress and prosperity. But by making economics machine-like Hoover had violated the very natural laws he purported to study. Not surprisingly, the deformed progeny had grown "beyond our natural and normal growth." Hoover and his Republican brethren had birthed a Frankenstein monster—a deformed beast incapable of surviving in a world where "economic laws are not made by nature. They are made by human beings." Thus did Roosevelt reembody economic recovery—away from a misanthropic intellectual elite to "the kind of economics that you and I and the average man and woman talk."[41]

Such talk took the form of a story in which Roosevelt "touches on" and "looks at" events that culminated in the depression. Importantly, he medicalized one of the chief causes of it—stock market speculation. The common folk were not fully responsible for the stock market crash since they were "under the spell of delirious speculation." Such delirium was precipitated by government policies and the unscrupulous motives of banks and corporations. Roosevelt concluded, "Those are the facts. Why blink at them?"[42] Again, he called attention to his acute vision and his ability to cast a nearly blinding light on the dark secrets of finance.

But Roosevelt implored his audience to engage in a different type of seeing, one equally about facts and bodies. "Translate that [the depression] into human terms. *See* how the events of the past three years have *come home* to specific groups of people: first, the group dependent on industry; second, the group dependent on agriculture; third, . . . the people who are called 'small investors and depositors.'" Roosevelt was quite literal with respect to the domesticity of the depression: "*Go into* the home of the business man. He knows what the tariff has done for him. *Go into* the home of the factory worker. He knows why goods do not move. *Go into* the home of the farmer. He knows how the tariff has helped to ruin him. At last our *eyes are open"* (emphasis added).[43] Not only did Roosevelt put a human face and a human body on the depression, but he also did so in a manner that emphasized his physical prowess; he had gone into these homes to view firsthand the embodied economic effects of Republican rule.

Having impugned the Hoover administration, Roosevelt made the transition to his position on such economic topics as credit, taxation, unemployment, agriculture, and tariffs—each of which was articulated, to varying degrees, in physical terms. Nearly four months earlier, on April 7, Roosevelt had called for economic policies "that put their faith once more in the forgotten man at the bottom of the economic pyramid." Many, including Smith, reacted virulently to Roosevelt's blatant class appeal. By July, Roosevelt had changed his position considerably, and again he linked a policy issue (credit) to a physical ability: "All of these groups, each and every one, the top of the pyramid and the bottom of the pyramid, must be considered together. . . . Statesmanship and vision, my friends, require relief to all at the same time."[44] Vision, of course, was occluded by sitting down. By standing tall, perhaps taller than any of his contemporaries, Roosevelt could see the entire class spectrum. Such acute vision was vital if he was to relieve the ills that afflicted the entire body politic.

That Roosevelt was literal about his role as national doctor, as Suzanne Daughton details, is attested to by his frequent use of medical terminology to describe the New Deal.[45] But even before becoming president Roosevelt spoke of his willingness to make house calls and the physical intimacy such visits would entail: "I shall be able to make a number of short visits to several parts of the Nation. My trips will have as their first objective the study at first *hand,* from the *lips* of men and women of all parties and all occupations, of the actual conditions and needs of every part of an interdependent country" (emphasis added).[46] In the span of eleven years, the roles had been reversed: The physically crippled had come to "take care of" a sick nation.

But Roosevelt could walk, or so he implied as he spoke about taxation: "I know something of taxes. For three long years I have been *going up and down* this country preaching that Government—Federal and State and local—costs too much. I shall not stop that preaching" (emphasis added).[47] This admission is curious. Why not, "I have been traveling across this country"—a much more standard locution? One explanation is that "going up and down" the country suggests a much more strenuous physical activity. Roosevelt had climbed steep hills and descended deep valleys, a perilous journey for anyone, and yet he had been doing it for "three long years." Roosevelt, the peripatetic preacher, may have been long suffering, but he was no sedentary cripple.

Roosevelt returned to a familiar set of physical images as he moved to discuss the problem of unemployment. He first proposed to "take *definite steps* to shorten the working day and the working week" (emphasis added). He also suggested a massive reforestation plan—a plan that would eventually materialize into the Civilian Conservation Corps (CCC) on March 19, 1933. The plan was necessary since "we *face* a future of soil erosion and timber famine. It is *clear* that economic *foresight* and immediate employment *march hand in hand* in the call for the reforestation of these vast areas" (emphasis added).[48] Here, Roosevelt and the unemployed marched (not walked) in unison toward the vision that he saw so clearly.

His physical rhetoric extended into the realm of agriculture, where he hoped to lighten "some of the impoverishing burdens from his [the farmer's] back." One means of addressing those burdens involved what was known as domestic allotment, a measure that promoted planning of agricultural production. Such a relatively drastic measure, Roosevelt reassured his listeners, would be "a desirable *first step* in the reconstruction of agriculture. . . . It will serve in great measure in the *long run* to remove the pall of a surplus" (emphasis added). As for the wording of a bill, "the Democratic Party *stands* ready to be guided by whatever the responsible farm groups themselves agree on" (emphasis added).[49] Roosevelt, in other words, would not take the emergency lying down; instead, he would offer farmers the same sort of visible and active leadership he would provide to people dealing with the problems of credit, taxation, and unemployment.

In June of 1930, fifteen months after proposing some protectionist agricultural legislation, Hoover signed into law the Smoot-Hawley Tariff Act. As Richard Hofstadter notes, the autarkic legislation "was a virtual declaration of economic war on the rest of the world."[50] Though he refused to call it by name, Roosevelt alluded to the putatively Republican measure toward the close of the address. And, perhaps predictably, the imagery again suggested sexual deviance. Roosevelt chronicled the "one great, simple, crystal-pure fact" that the nation "has been led by the Republican leaders to erect an impregnable barbed wire entanglement around its borders through the instrumentality of tariffs." "Erect" and "impregnable" are too close for metaphorical comfort. The ultimate effect seemed to involve a sublimation of the sexual urge, resulting in a hostile economic response that has "isolated us from all other human beings in all the rest of the round world." Physical and economic isolation and repression were the tangible results, a situation inimical to "the restoration of the trade of the world."[51]

Roosevelt's peroration includes perhaps the best-remembered political label in the history of twentieth-century American public address. In what was considered a throwaway line by his advisors, Roosevelt stated, "I pledge you, I pledge myself, to a new deal for the American people." Thus was born the Rooseveltian New Deal—despite the fact that Roosevelt never offered a consistent, systematic set of policy objectives. But to remember the peroration only for this contractual promise misses the physical culmination of the address in which Roosevelt's listeners rise, walk, and view tomorrow's landscape with their new leader. In keeping with the text's emphasis on standing, seeing, and walking, Roosevelt ended most appropriately: "Never before in modern history have the essential differences between the two major American political parties *stood out* in such *striking contrast* as they do today. Republican leaders not only have failed in material things, they have failed in *national vision.* . . . They have pointed out *no path* for the people below to *climb back to* places of security and safety in our American life" (emphasis added).[52] They were thus the "false prophets" of prosperity, the reprobates responsible for leading the American people along "the easy road without toil." Economic recovery for Roosevelt was premised on an ability to see the future and on a visceral physicality in which walking without toil simply would not suffice; recovery involved using all of one's limbs. Roosevelt was not merely using figurative language; the political campaign was indeed "a call to arms."

According to at least two important sources, Franklin Roosevelt's dramatic flight and speech to the Democratic National Convention achieved the desired effect. On July 4, the *New York Times* editorialized, "Governor Roosevelt put into his appearance and address before the Chicago Convention something of the breeziness that went naturally with his flight through the air. The dash and vigor which he had shown by setting out for Chicago in an airplane also marked his speech." The editorial writers concluded that "the Democratic candidate for the Presidency is bringing a fresh and eager mind and an ardent spirit to the work which his party has placed in his hands."[53] The following day, Claude G. Bowers opined in the *New York Journal,* "The speech of Roosevelt was a triumph. The delegates found before them a virile figure, physically strong, . . . a militant figure with an eagerness to fight."[54]

In the immediate aftermath of his triumph at the Democratic National Convention, there were many who strongly advised Roosevelt to wage a Hardingesque "front-porch" campaign, where he might periodically deliver speeches via radio from either Hyde Park or Albany. Roosevelt not only spurned their advice, as we show in the next chapter, but he would wage his most active campaign to date, taking his body once again on the road. It alone seemed to offer the most compelling proof that Roosevelt was in fact presidential timber.

7 "A Satisfactory Embodiment"

Just like Roosevelt's convention speeches and appearances in 1924 and 1928, the automobile campaign of 1928, the $500,000 life insurance policy of 1930, and the Earle Looker *Liberty Magazine* article of 1931, his dramatic flight of July 2, 1932, likely persuaded many of his fitness for elected office. But by no means did it persuade all. If anything, the whispering campaign moved to a sustained crescendo during the summer and fall of 1932. This situation should not surprise us, though, given that Herbert Hoover and many others in the Republican party openly hoped for a Roosevelt candidacy. Their position was that now the country would see the real Roosevelt, and the country had best be warned of what his condition really meant. "Millions of people are going to try to throw out the strong Herbert Hoover and put in his place a man who cannot arise from his chair unassisted and who can only shuffle and drag his feet instead of walk," intoned James H. MacLafferty, three weeks after the Democratic National Convention. "They had better look out."[1]

MacLafferty's sentiments, of course, are those of a Hoover shill and can thus be taken accordingly. But his rather dismissive view of the candidate's health was not the belief solely of the Republican party; many Democrats shared his concerns. Adding to their concerns was a plan, developed largely by Roosevelt himself, to actively show his body across the country via train. In an article penned by Louis Howe after the general election, he described how "a great majority of the Governor's advisors were strongly opposed to his making a tour to the coast and back." Out of presidential power now for twelve long years, key Democratic operatives did not want to gamble the party's executive auspices away on an unnecessary and risky trip. "A delegation of men who were in real power in party counsels [*sic*] waited on him in Albany to persuade him from such a course," Howe noted. This delegation feared "that the carefully disseminated propaganda as to the Governor's health must have some foundation, and that he would be unable to stand the rigors of a grueling campaign." Howe claims further that such a fear "never entered the minds of the Governor's intimate friends."[2] Jim

Farley's recollection was different: "The newspapers, well wishers, friends, etc., all tried to dissuade Roosevelt from his determination to made [sic] that first trip West; but he insisted upon it."[3]

Regardless of who was actually urging Roosevelt not to make the strenuous train trip, the three major campaign architects—Howe, Farley, and Moley—all agreed on Roosevelt's motive. Said Farley, "He thought he should prove to the West that he was not a sick man and he emerged from that trip a stronger candidate than when he went on it." Howe stated the matter even more succinctly: "The Governor realized that the best answer to the question as to his health was himself."[4] His body was simply the best proof that Roosevelt could muster—better than radio, better than press conferences, and certainly better than any surrogate. Staying home at Hyde Park or Albany could be perceived as having something to hide, and thus a stay-at-home campaign strategy could potentially foment even more whispering. More than forty years after the campaign, Moley responded to the question of whether Roosevelt had taken the campaign tour of the West in order to prove his physical fitness for the presidency. Moley was emphatic: "Oh, yes, there is no doubt about that, although I don't remember that it was specifically mentioned by him, but he wanted to show himself as being a man of vigor and vitality and wasn't hampered in any way by his physical infirmity."[5]

It is clear that those behind the scenes knew Roosevelt's true motives for the trip and expressed that knowledge accordingly. Not so with the candidate; raising the health issue in conversations about politics was very much verboten. Howe noted Roosevelt's publicly petulant reason for heading west: "'Gentlemen, I have listened carefully to your arguments, against my going to the coast and back or even as far as Chicago. . . . There is, however, one reason in favor of my going which has not been brought to your attention, and that reason is—I want to.'"[6] It is true that Roosevelt genuinely loved campaigning, but those closest to him knew that after eleven years, he was not going to leave the final four months to chance. To borrow from Farley's stock of metaphors, he would go down (or up) swinging.

But Roosevelt also knew that he could not be everywhere at once. In the pre-television, pre-satellite era, campaigning for public office was truly a pedestrian affair. Being in Topeka meant that he could not be in Omaha, and so he needed some type of influence other than his own body to stop the whispering. Much of that influence was his own recent past; the pivotal public maneuverings, in other words, of the past eight years were brought forward as evidence of the candidate's sound health. The past chapters in Roosevelt's recovery were now brought to bear, sometimes cumulatively, sometimes singularly, as the climactic moment in his political recrudescence neared.

Nearly a month and a half before the planned West Coast trip, Farley was attempting to preempt Republicans on the issue of Roosevelt's health. His "proof" rested with the recent convention, so he told listeners of WABC, "'I do not believe that anybody who saw him when he addressed the convention after flying from Albany to Chicago has any doubt of his physical endurance.'"[7] Only a few weeks after the convention, it was obvious that Roosevelt had had reasons other than political tradition and money for flying to Chicago. The following day, on August 1, the *New York Times* seemed to be warming up to the Howe-Farley-Moley party line: the only way for Roosevelt to end the whispering was to display "great industry and activity every day." They also reported optimistically that the candidate was "preparing to make a vigorous and aggressive campaign, which should convince even the most suspicious or malicious that he is able to rise completely above the slight bodily handicap."[8]

Examining the primary and secondary source material related to the campaign, we found it difficult to conclude positively whether those "most suspicious" or "malicious" regarding Roosevelt's health were predominantly male or female. Bodily disability clearly had a gendered dimension to it, as we have maintained, but that dimension has only been considered from the vantage point of the disabled—in this case, Roosevelt. If we pause to consider the subject rather than the object, two documents that survive from the campaign suggest that Roosevelt's disability weighed very heavily, perhaps conspicuously so, on the minds of some women voters. In a one-page flier headlined "Three Reasons Why Every Woman Should Vote for Roosevelt and Garner," two very traditional concerns of women are featured: the safety of children and the sanctity of marriage and the home. In other words, monogamy and heterosexuality are lauded as virtues that Roosevelt and Garner embody and would defend. But there is a third reason for women to vote for Franklin Roosevelt—and it had nothing to do with the vice-presidential candidate. Appearing first in order of priority on the flier was the following: "Roosevelt has known pain and hardship. He has fought a courageous and winning battle to health. He can understand the man and woman who is today struggling against terrific odds and he can be trusted to put heart as well as mind into the battle."[9] As opposed to men who might be inclined to view Roosevelt's disability within a less than masculine frame, women were recommended to see it as a humanizing, empathic factor in a Roosevelt presidency. Ironically, Roosevelt's disability enabled him to become more feeling and more sensitive, someone whose disabled body had helped create a more rounded mind. This candidate was indeed whole—the politics of the Great Depression required the head (typically gendered masculine) and the heart (typically gendered feminine). This wholeness was the foremost reason for the recently franchised female to cast her ballot for the Democrats. And just for safe measure, Roosevelt's virile heterosexuality was carefully underscored in reasons two and three.

A similar concern for Roosevelt's health appears in a document for those women actively campaigning for Roosevelt and Garner. The Democratic National Campaign Committee (DNCC) provided its women's division with a lengthy speaker's kit of "suggested answers to Republican assertions." If in fact Democratic women were speaking to Republican women, the foremost concern was Roosevelt's fitness for office. Republican assertion number one reads: "Franklin D. Roosevelt is unfit physically to assume the trying duties of the presidency." The "answer" suggested by the committee was to point out two recent pieces of evidence to the contrary: the $500,000 life insurance policy offered to Roosevelt in 1930 and the medical report issued by Drs. Hibbs, Lambert, and Kennedy in 1931 under the auspices of the Earle Looker challenge published in *Liberty Magazine.* The conclusion was simple: "In spite of this disability of the legs, Mr. Roosevelt is in topnotch physical condition."[10] Matters of policy clearly were subordinate, at least in the Democrats' mind, to the female voter.

Of course the health issue was not exclusively a male or female issue; many of the fliers not targeted to a specific sex addressed the issue in some detail and with some urgency. In a flier distributed under the auspices of the DNCC and titled "Half a Million Life Insurance," a torso photograph of the candidate is surrounded by thirteen pamphlets, each featuring a difference life insurance company policy. The implication was clear: Roosevelt's health was being vouchsafed by some of the nation's most reputable insurers. The flier made sure to drive home the point: "No physical tests are more searching than life insurance examinations on which money is risked." In large, bold, italicized letters was this statement: "They found that Franklin D. Roosevelt is sound, healthy and physically fit." As with the women's campaign literature, Earle Looker's handiwork also made an appearance: "Three eminent doctors . . . examined Franklin D. Roosevelt last year at the request of Liberty Magazine." In the same large, bold, italicized type font, the flier reported that the doctors found "Franklin D. Roosevelt's health and powers of endurance are such as to allow him to meet any demand of private and public life." At the bottom of the flier, readers are urged to "Stop the Whispering Campaign. Elect a Strong Leader—Franklin D. Roosevelt."[11]

Perhaps not surprisingly, even the "Campaign Book of the Democratic Party Candidates and Issues 1932" features Roosevelt's return to good health. Again, the $500,000 life insurance policy and the Looker-inspired medical examination are highlighted. This publication also featured Roosevelt's record as governor, which of course was a record marked first and foremost by good health: "The story of his governorship is one of a man steadily growing in mental, physical and spiritual strength." That story also featured such onerous tasks as dictating a heavy correspondence, conducting dozens of conferences, writing and giving speeches, and working extensively on policy proposals. Not to be overlooked was the candidate's extensive travel, "from 20,000 to 30,000 miles annually." Such travel "exhausts those who go with him—but he seems never exhausted." A final testament to Roosevelt's stamina, vitality, and general good health was the now quasi-legendary flight to Chicago: "The moment word of his nomination flashed out Roosevelt electrified the convention and bewildered the whisperers who charged he was a sick man by his spectacular airplane flight from Albany to Chicago."[12] With terms such as "flashed out," "electrified," and "spectacular," it is hard to believe that Roosevelt did not leap to the convention in a single bound. But such hyperbole on the part of the DNCC also implies a corresponding anxiety. Why exaggerate if there were no doubts? In another DNCC-sponsored pamphlet supposedly dealing with Roosevelt's political record, that record was again largely subordinated to the candidate's robust health. But instead of marshaling evidence to quiet the whispering, this pamphlet presumptively dispatched it altogether by making it a part of Roosevelt's past: "The 'whispering campaign' of his enemies which sought to picture him as a 'helpless cripple' was promptly met by the securing of over half a million dollars' worth of life insurance policies at the lowest rates." Two sections later, the pamphlet boasts that Roosevelt was "Stronger than Hoover."[13]

But Roosevelt was not confident that the casual reader would believe the campaign propaganda, the disembodied words on a page. And so precisely at 11 P.M. on September 12, 1932, The *Roosevelt Special* departed from Albany, headed for the West Coast. On his way there and back, the candidate would deliver some fifty-six speeches in twenty days. On some days, he would deliver six speeches. The function of these speeches was not necessarily policy; Roosevelt would rarely say more than a sentence or two about a specific issue, depending on what part of the country he was in. Instead, several times a day, he would go through the terribly arduous process of strapping on his heavy leg braces, and with the performance he had perfected at Warm Springs, he would "walk" to the back platform of the last car and allow the hundreds, many times thousands, of people assembled to see him. Unlike the gubernatorial race in 1928, Roosevelt did not joke with his audience about his purportedly enfeebled body; perhaps he simply wanted to avoid making the issue potentially bigger than it already was. The closest that he came to an admission of motive occurred in Goodland, Kansas, just three days into the trip. To an audience estimated at one thousand people, Roosevelt gave this greeting: "It's fine to see you! We are going through the country doing a very simple thing: we are showing ourselves to you, and we are talking very simply and plainly to the voters in most of the United States."[14] Had Herbert Hoover or any other candidate made such a curious admission, the response might have been one of confusion. Not so with Roosevelt; many people, especially those out west who had seen only photographs of the candidate, did want to give the candidate a careful once-over—especially after the rampant whispering.

The *Brooklyn Daily Eagle* well captured the "typical" campaign stop along the nation's rails: "The train comes to a dead stop when the rear end is opposite the station. The Governor emerges from his private car on the arm of his eldest son, James. He walks to the railing at the back of the observation platform and acknowledges the greetings of the crowd." Typically, Roosevelt would say to the assembled masses, "'I am just out here to look, learn, and listen,'" and then "he repeats a few phrases from his speech of the night before." The correspondents also understood the extra-discursive work being done: "The whole idea of the Governor's managers is to let the people see him during the day and hear him at night over the radios while the vision of his large, handsome features and broad shoulders is still in their minds."[15]

While the great majority of Roosevelt's speeches on this trip were extemporaneous in nature, he and his advisors realized that he would have to do more than merely "show" himself to an inquisitive audience. Reassuring the public that he had a healthy body was, after all, only the first step toward a possible Roosevelt presidency. There was also the matter of the Great Depression and what Roosevelt would do differently than Hoover. With the aid of several influential academics and politicians, Moley organized nine major policy-oriented speeches, on topics ranging from the tariff and the regulation of public utilities to farming and transportation. One of the things that unites most of these speeches, aside from their status as policy pronouncements, is a subtle but extremely important rhetorical characterization of the economy. Instead of simply referring to "the economy" in a nonmetaphorical manner, Roosevelt and his advisors adopted, whether purposefully or not, the dominant metaphor of the day in talking about the economic situation—that of bodily health and sickness.

Metaphor, by definition, invokes a comparison between two unlike things—in this case the economic reality as a healthy or sick body. That Roosevelt had successfully convalesced from a most debilitating illness, we argue, engendered a rhetorical authority that worked greatly to his advantage. Long before Franklin Roosevelt fancied himself as "Dr. New Deal," he incorporated a medical lexicon, a body economics so to speak, that greatly minimized the extent of his own physical disability. A sick and prostrate people needed a healer, and who better to fulfill that role than a recovering paralytic who knew something of sickness, pain, and hardship? Serving as a healer was the medical role of a lifetime, and the opportunity to do so had come at a most fortuitous political time.

That the sick body had emerged as the dominant metaphorical understanding of the economic situation by 1932 was, perhaps, no mere rhetorical accident. Herbert Hoover had initially employed the metaphor of a storm, perhaps indicative of the violent, but brief, ferocity of the October, 1929, stock market crash. That metaphor eventually became obsolete because the carnage from the crash, plus economic events abroad, stayed around far longer than any storm could hold together. Perhaps the economic situation was caused by something far less random, something far more fundamental to the human condition. On April 23, 1930, the editors of the weekly magazine called *The Business Week* raised the specter of the business "slump" (not yet a depression) "as an inescapable consequence of some original economic sin, and prosperity can be restored only by a duly prolonged process of penance."[16] But less than three months later even the "God-punishing-greed" account of the economic situation was being mixed with more anthropocentric terminology. The editors lamented the activities of the statistical "high priests" and economic "father-confessors" who "grimly present the castor-oil bottle and pour us daily a large dose." Instead of a "mere resort to 'drugs,' 'nostrums,' and 'panaceas,' which are sinful," the business cycle "must be yielded its pound of flesh." The "body politic simply needed to go back again to a plain diet of pork and beans, without any tomato sauce."[17]

A logical question at this point is, why equate the economy and the human body? What in the economic context of 1930 and following enabled the human body and its ailments to become the dominant metaphorical interpretation of the era known as the Great Depression? We offer two possibilities. First, a decrease in income ultimately locates itself in the body: less income to feed hungry and eventually malnourished bodies; less income to clothe, bathe, and warm cold and dirty bodies; and less income to heal sick bodies. Thus does economic collapse come to be felt, literally, at the most elemental of levels. Second, Elaine Scarry offers the human need for the familiar and known as a reason for the appearance of the body in times of uncertainty and doubt. Whenever there is a crisis of belief in society, "the sheer material factualness of the human body will be borrowed to lend that cultural construct [in this case, capitalism] the aura of 'realness' and 'certainty.'"[18] In an era of grave doubt about the endurance and even the possibility of capitalism, the human body and its ailments provided a palpable realness, and thus reassurance.

A logical consequence of the metaphor, though, involved diagnosing the malady adversely affecting the economic body, and it was here that great disagreement was expressed by the nation's writers. In an article titled

"Doctors, Economists, and the Depression," F. W. Taussig participated in the "autopsy of the economic fatality."[19] Since the economic body, he argued, required change and dynamism, national planning under the aegis of socialism would rid it of its disorder and return it to good health. The editors of the *New Republic* diagnosed the ills as having been caused by "the lingering tumor of an overgrown tribute to capital charges." To excise that tumor and "get capitalism on its feet again," a surgical operation was needed which "would of course require many kinds of anesthetics and stringent controls."[20]

Some writers, such as Roger W. Babson, even went so far as to literalize the metaphor. The cause behind the contraction of income was that "consumers are tired out physically"; they had "reached the limits of their physical capacity." He argued further that a time would come "when we must recognize the depression as physiological and curable only as we correct the universal fatigue and physical exhaustion." All that was needed was the "unbeatable prescription of a sound mind in a sound body."[21] In less than two months, Babson had changed his diagnosis—to the point of reversing it: "The symptom of modern depression is overproduction."[22] Like Babson in the first of the two articles cited here, James Bayard Clark also literalized the metaphor, but he did so cautiously. "Why should not a doctor put the social body through the same sort of examination and testing that he applies to the human body when it is sick?" Clark asked. He questioned further, "Is not this well-being based squarely upon the physical health and happiness of the individual parts of the social body?" The answer, of course, was yes, which allowed an isomorphism between healthy bodies and healthy economies: "Advanced physiological and biochemical knowledge makes it perfectly clear that an exact balance must be maintained in the reciprocal activity of these smaller bodies if the physical body as a whole is to function normally and economically." This "exact balance" that Clark was advocating was a euphemism for redistributing wealth, which would lead to a "hygiene of wealth."[23]

For many writers, however, the problem was not a disease or a sickness; rather, it was the surgeons and the physicians. Louis T. McFadden of the *Saturday Evening Post* noted that "our financial patient had, with sheer lack of proper preparation on the part of some of the attending physicians and surgeons, been permitted to lapse into a perilous unconsciousness." In order to revitalize the nation's "monetary corpuscles," it was incumbent on all citizens, not just the experts, to assist "our patient back to health, in getting him back upon his feet again."[24] The famed journalist Walter Lippmann was also not immune from the metaphor, and, like McFadden, he laid much of the blame on the physicians: "The medicine was never strong enough by the time the doctor made up his mind to administer it."[25] The editors of the

Saturday Evening Post argued that the doctors had actually done too much: "No matter how much the quack doctors and charlatans howl, there is no way for the wound to heal except as wounds do heal in Nature and that is gradually." Since the "cells of a diseased body usually heal" on their own, "it would have been far better if we had sense enough never to catch the disease in the first place."[26] The editors of *The Business Week* sounded a similar noninterventionist note: "Business life has the quality of all nature: it is self-restorative, self-healing. Most of its ailments and misfortunes are self-limited: the doctors can do nothing more than give natural economic forces a chance to operate to repair waste and restore health."[27]

William Trufant Foster speculated on the "physical" causes of the depression, asking, "Is that [unbalanced production, thus income disparity] the real cause of our paralysis, or is it, as other doctors of business believe, the decline in foreign trade?" He, too, thought that the metaphor—in this case "depression"—needed literalizing. Unlike Clark and Babson, Foster saw no physical deficiency in the patient; therefore "the trouble must be psychological. . . . Mental states have far more to do with this depression than physical facts."[28]

There were many others who voiced a similar view of the nation's economic misfortunes. Chief among them was the Philadelphia-based Business Progressive Association, which was featured in an article that ran in *The World Tomorrow* in March of 1931. According to the article's author, Nelson H. Cruikshank, the association members believed that "the disorder is not real—it is a state of mind." And while the consequences of such a disorder may have made people feel "as if the cause were real," "the pains must not be dwelt upon as they only serve to magnify the mental state that is at the bottom of the disorder." Because the problem was mental, a state of mind, the "remedy" was quite simple: "Use of the new instrument the present age has discovered: What President Wilson called 'pitiless publicity.'" A nonphysical solution needed only compelling rhetoric to heal the body economic. Perhaps most interesting of all, Cruikshank noted that the group's beliefs and practices were not unique; none other than "the President himself lends dignity to this practice."[29]

Herbert Hoover would in fact argue for the better part of three years that a mental condition—what he termed "confidence"—was largely responsible for the nation's economic fortunes and misfortunes.[30] If he could only persuade the nation that the economy would be better in the near future, then that economy would actually improve in the present. Like the great English economist John Maynard Keynes, Hoover was aware of the many macroeconomic powers of the "animal spirits." People simply would neither spend their money nor put it in banks if they lacked confidence. Confidence also appealed to Herbert Hoover at the level of governance;

confidence, he figured, needed "only" persuasion, not legislation. Roosevelt did not necessarily disagree with Hoover, but he would adopt, as we detail below, a much more body-centered approach to the nation's maladies; he would also use this approach when recommending cures.

While the sickness was variously diagnosed as mental or physical, there were many who simply admitted that they did not know what had caused the problem. As the Great Depression neared its nadir in the summer of 1932, economic historian Edwin F. Gay lamented, "No one, however skilled, really knows the character of or the specific cure for what some practitioners diagnose as a wasting disease."[31] The editors of the *Saturday Evening Post* had grown weary with diagnosis ennui: "Uncle Sam limps along through the depression. . . . There is a pitch on every corner and a present wrapped up with every bottle of cure-all offered."[32]

A great advantage that Roosevelt held over Hoover as the general campaign got under way was that he had witnessed Hoover's repeated rhetorical failures. He had watched as the president repeatedly told the press and the public that all that was needed for prosperity to return was a change of mind, a return to confidence. Roosevelt did not necessarily disagree, as a speech he gave before heading west makes clear. At Columbus, Ohio, on August 20, he stated unequivocally that "restored confidence in the actions and statements of Executive authority is indispensable." Roosevelt specified further the type of confidence that was needed: "The confidence that the administration has asked us as individual citizens to have in ourselves is not enough. The kind of confidence we most need is confidence in the integrity, the soundness, the liberalism, the vision, and the old-fashioned horse sense of our national leadership."[33] As he ventured west Roosevelt set out to earn that confidence, a confidence that was based not only on policy but also on his physical ability to lead a nation that fancied itself prostrate from illness. Confidence in Roosevelt's physical abilities would accrue incrementally at each campaign stop, with each fastening on of the leg braces, with each appearance out on the train's back platform with members of his family and local and regional politicians. But Roosevelt also borrowed from the dominant vernacular of the day in diagnosing the economic situation. It just so happened that that vernacular greatly equalized things; a crippled nation was now to meet its crippled leader, who knew something of recovery.

Roosevelt's first major policy address took place on September 14, in Topeka. Nearly twenty thousand people, mostly farmers, braved the sweltering heat to hear the self-declared farmer talk about agriculture. Roosevelt advanced his agricultural program with the interrelated imagery of unity and health. Agriculture, he argued, could not be segregated from the rest of the nation's economy, particularly industry. As in his "Concert of Interests" speech of April 18, Roosevelt claimed that "our economic life today is a seamless web." Notice that Roosevelt did not use the more commonplace construction "our economy"; he said "our economic life." Economic interdependence was inextricably tied to the nation's collective life and health: "We cannot have independence in its true sense unless we take full account of our interdependence in order to provide a balanced economic well being for every citizen of the country."[34] Economic health, "balance," and interdependence would be achieved by a "unity of planning," as opposed to the Hoover administration's "scattering of efforts." Such all-encompassing planning measures would provide a "cure" or "remedy," whereas Hoover had merely prescribed "drugs" as a short-term economic palliative. Roosevelt's program would thus eradicate the illness altogether.

Perhaps the most important first step toward economic well-being, though, was a belief that one's health could improve. Roosevelt advised that "the farmer's hope for the future must rest upon *the policy and the spirit* in which his case is considered. The essence of this question [of agricultural relief] comes down to a matter of keeping faith with American agriculture" (emphasis added).[35] But Roosevelt went one step further; he invited his listeners in the farming community to join him in a "profession of faith." Their faith and, hence, future health were partially ensured through the incantatory powers of language.

Three days later at Salt Lake City, Roosevelt further elaborated on the relationship between interdependence and health as it related to the railroad industry. As he had at Topeka, Roosevelt made a complex topic comprehensible largely by attributing human characteristics to it. His stated goal was to improve "the health of these great arteries of commerce" to the point where they could "stand on their own feet." At the time the railroad industry suffered from an "epidemic" of illnesses and was being "strangled half to death" by a lack of planning. Like the situation in agriculture, the lack of concerted planning had "unbalanc[ed] the system of things." The remedy was simply one of "reordering" and "coordination": "The individual railroads should be regarded as points of a national transportation system. . . . Each rail service should fit into and be coordinated with other rail services and with other forms of transportation."[36]

But Roosevelt noted again that revitalized economic health was not premised solely on the policies that his administration would pursue; recovery was also contingent on belief. "We still have before us," he said, "as had those who settled this great West, battles with hunger, battles with human selfishness and, what is more important, the battle with our own spirits, seeking, in the face of discouragement, the means of restoration and relief."[37] Roosevelt's call for people to battle themselves appears to fly in the face of his pronouncement at Columbus, namely, that confidence came from without, not solely from within. And, unlike his message at Topeka, in Salt Lake City Roosevelt did not explicitly offer an external agent to nurse the sick patient back to health; instead, people could turn inward for strength by drawing on "the hardihood of the pioneer."

At Seattle, Roosevelt continued to invoke the role of omniscient country doctor to assuage fears that economic health might not return. Hoover, not by deliberate intent but through insufficient understanding, had unleashed a deadly "poison" in the economic bloodstream with the imposition of high tariffs. Roosevelt's "remedy" was simply to "barter" or talk with each country and, thereby, eliminate barriers to trade.[38] Roosevelt's "poison" metaphor had two very important entailments. First, the people were not responsible for spreading the poison; it had been loosed by an out-of-touch president. Second, given that Roosevelt labeled the Smoot-Hawley Tariff Act as poisonous, it would seem logical for him to renounce it altogether. Yet Roosevelt's proposed solution—reciprocal tariff agreements—would only lessen the poison's toxicity; it would not remove it from the bloodstream.

It was also in Seattle that Roosevelt did something out of the ordinary; instead of meeting with strictly political groups and addressing primarily Democratic audiences, the candidate paid a visit to crippled children at the Children's Orthopedic Hospital. In addressing his young audience, Roosevelt said, "'Some of you children know it's a little difficult for me to stand on my own feet, the same as many of you.'" He also told the children that he was an expert swimmer. In response, the *Seattle Times* reported that one child said that "'if he can swim, maybe I can too.'" The visit, the newspaper reported, "was scheduled at the request of Governor Roosevelt."[39]

As the *Roosevelt Special* headed back east after a swing through California and Arizona, Roosevelt also attempted to counter accusations that he would be bested at the international bargaining table. Not surprisingly, he contextualized the charges within the sphere of health and sickness: "Do you believe that our early instincts for successful barter have degenerated or atrophied? I do not think so. I have confidence . . . that the red blood of the men who sailed our Yankee clipper ships . . . still courses in our veins. I cannot picture Uncle Sam as a supine, white-livered, flabby-muscled old man cooling his heels in the shade of our tariff walls."[40]

The image of a prostrate man, someone whose once strong legs had "degenerated or atrophied" was one that Roosevelt "could not picture"—despite the reservations of many and despite the fact that he drew a most convincing picture. The implication was clear: Roosevelt was blind to his own handicap; he was strong enough to take on "our more experienced friends" at the bargaining table. Thus did Roosevelt embody the very possibility of America's renewed economic health; it was nascent within his own crippled body. His audience five days earlier at the Hollywood Bowl in Los Angeles would likely have reached a similar conclusion. He began his informal remarks by drawing attention to his physical and mental health: "It has been a long trip, my friends, but unlike most long trips those of us who have been making it have left behind any feelings of fatigue of the mind or body."[41] The word "body" had been penciled in the margin, jotted down in Roosevelt's signature script.

Roosevelt gave his last major address of the trip on October 2, in Detroit. In it, he chronicled how progressive measures such as better public health, worker's compensation, old age insurance, and mental hygiene had prevented the spread of poverty. But poverty, he added, was not unlike a disease: "We have got beyond the point in modern civilization of merely trying to fight an epidemic of disease by taking care of the victims after they are stricken. . . . We seek to prevent it and the attack on poverty is not very unlike the attack on disease." Medicalizing poverty served at least three important rhetorical functions. First, it reduced the complex social forces associated with poverty to a universal locus of causality, one in which science held potential "remedies." Second, poverty, like certain diseases, came from without; people were indiscriminately infected with poverty and were not, therefore, culpable for something beyond their immediate control. Roosevelt noted that "the causes of poverty in the main are beyond the control of any one individual."[42] Third, medicalizing poverty thrust the unwitting victims into an extremely acquiescent role. Without supervision and treatment, they could not exorcise their symptoms. They were essentially forced to follow the omniscient doctor's prescriptions and then allow nature to run its course.

Roosevelt contextualized progressive cures for poverty as a movement forward—as a "path of faith," a "path of hope," and a "path of love" that culminated in "the path of social justice." And, as he had indicated most recently in his July 2 acceptance speech and as far back as his "Quo Vadis?" address, Roosevelt would lead the way. After repeating "we cannot go back" six times in one paragraph, he concluded, "There are a lot of new steps to take. It is not a question of just not going back. It is a question also of not standing still. . . . The problem of unemployment in the long run can be and shall be solved by the human race."[43]

While Roosevelt was busy persuading the electorate of his fitness for office, he had others, clearly rhetorical surrogates, tackling the health issue head on. Sen. Royal S. Copeland of New York addressed it in a speech to the American Hospital Association meeting in Detroit: "'His lameness never has borne any possible relationship to his mental welfare and has proved to be no more than a trifling physical handicap to a very active person.'"[44] And, the senator added, "'His expectancy of life is greater than President

Hoover's [a claim that proved to be off by nearly thirty years]."[45] Francis P. Garvan, head of the Chemical Foundation, excoriated those still whispering about the candidate's health. In a speech of September 18, he stated, "'Men and women, "not playing the game," are whispering false rumors about his health, to the effect that he will not be able to discharge his duties as President and that he will not live out his term.'"[46] Roosevelt's old boss in the Wilson administration, Secretary of the Navy Josephus Daniels, also came to the candidate's defense. In an article penned for the *Saturday Evening Post,* Daniels resorted to a scientistic rhetoric of facts to "prove" Roosevelt's fitness: "Two things have completely answered the whispering campaign . . . 1. The fact that conservative and nonpolitical life-insurance executives after thorough examination by medical experts, insured his life for $500,000, thus demonstrating by the highest testimony that physically he is sound." In presenting fact number two Daniels invoked the other standard proof, that Roosevelt "could fly to Chicago and stand for an hour before 30,000 people in the auditorium . . . and make his acceptance speech with mental and physical vigor." He had thus "silenced the whispering that [he] lacked virility and health and strength needed in the great office."[47]

Another Wilson administration colleague, the venerable "Colonel" Edward Mandell House, also rallied to the candidate's cause. His was a rhetoric premised upon experience: "I have met every president since Grant, and not one of them has had a stronger physique than Governor Roosevelt. I'll still go further than that: there has been only one who equaled him in physical prowess, and that was his illustrious relative, Theodore Roosevelt."[48]

If Copeland, Garvan, Daniels, and House were not enough, there was always the physician responsible for declaring the candidate's good health vis-à-vis the 1930 life insurance policy. The campaign released to the press a "private" letter from Dr. Edgar W. Beckwith shortly after Roosevelt received it. The doctor congratulated him "on the excellence of your physical condition," but he was "particularly impressed" by his "heart action and blood pressure both of which were entirely normal according to the standards for a man of your age." "Frankly," he concluded, "I have never before observed much complete degree of recovery in organic function and such a remarkable degree of recovery of muscles and limbs in an individual who had passed through an attack of infantile paralysis such as yours."[49] The health issue was truly going down to the wire; just a few weeks before election day and the campaign felt compelled to reiterate the results of a medical examination made more than two years ago.

The reports on the candidate that came back to campaign headquarters were mixed; obviously, all the whispering had not stopped. Adolf A. Berle, a campaign insider and Columbia University professor colleague of Moley and Tugwell, received a letter on the campaign from A. H. Levens of the Art

Metal Construction Company, with whom he had been corresponding. Levens reported to Berle what he had seen and heard: "The middle class citizen whom I have questioned seems to favor Hoover claiming that he could not have done any more than he did and they invariably add the remark about needing a healthy man in the Presidential Chair and that Roosevelt would not be physically capable of handling this position." This opinion clearly angered Levens: "It seems as tho this is so stereotyped that I am wondering whether a whispering campaign is not going on by the Republicans to spread those thoughts which I consider very unfair for some of the greatest men in history have been those who were physically weak."[50] But M. L. Wilson, an agricultural economics professor from Montana and consultant to the Roosevelt campaign, reported back to Moley that the *Roosevelt Special*'s stop in Montana had achieved the desired results, especially with the women voters: "The women are also saying that he appeared in splendid physical condition and that he must be a remarkable man to have overcome his unfortunate physical disabilities in such a complete manner."[51] That women would be more concerned than men about Roosevelt's disability should again give us pause as to the gendered implications of crippling disability.

Franklin Roosevelt was clearly pleased with the trip out west. So was Louis Howe, who had watched the trip from afar, at campaign headquarters in New York City. "No better answer to the fears those who doubted the Governor's strength could possibly have been found than the simple proof that the candidate himself was always fresh, always cheerful, strong of voice and strong of body," Howe wrote. Here was a man "who was having a wonderful time and enjoying every minute of it."[52] Whether it was because of his seemingly native love for campaigning or because of lingering concerns still being whispered about the country, Roosevelt decided that one train trip would not suffice. So, with his entourage in tow, the *Roosevelt Special* departed from Albany on October 18, bound for Syracuse and points west and south. In eight days the candidate would deliver twenty-three speeches in thirteen different states. And, again, the master metaphor featured in his speeches was that of health and sickness.

Perhaps the two most noteworthy uses of the metaphor were in Pittsburgh on October 19 and in Baltimore six days later. At Pittsburgh, Hoover was featured as the misanthropic doctor who had attributed America's economic collapse to foreign causes. Roosevelt mocked this "abroad" contention and wondered where, exactly, Hoover meant by "abroad," perhaps Abyssinia. Attributing the desperate economic situation to a foreign cause was "just like ascribing measles on our little boy to the spots on his chest, instead of to the contagious germ that he has picked up somewhere."[53] Roosevelt consistently used disease metaphors to address root causes and to reject the treatment of symptoms alone. They also functioned to indicate the random nature of contracting contagious diseases, if people were still inclined to link morality to illness. Thus might infantile paralysis be seen as a random event rather than moral retribution.

As he had at the convention in Chicago, Roosevelt adeptly linked sickness to the other side: "The air is . . . surcharged with Republican death-bed repentance on the subject of the economy, but it is too late." On the Democratic side, the healthy and vigorous side, Roosevelt promised the nation it would "start on the upward trail. We shall have built for economic recovery a firm footing, on a path that is broad, true and straight. Join me, and 'let's go!'"[54] Roosevelt was thus physically fit to lead the nation not along a mere road but a steep upward trail, and with his firm footing he was ready to lead others who would walk behind him.

The second prominent use of the health-and-sickness metaphor took place on October 25, in Baltimore. There, Roosevelt transformed Hoover from the hard-hearted deceiver of earlier speeches to the economic Antichrist. Incorporating the millennial drama of the Book of Revelation, Roosevelt likened Hoover and his henchmen to the Four Horsemen of the Apocalypse. The analogy, of course, cast Roosevelt in the role of economic savior: "I am waging a war in this campaign—a frontal attack—an onset—against the 'Four Horsemen' of the present Republican leadership: The Horsemen of Destruction, Delay, Deceit, Despair. And the time has come for us to marshal this 'Black Horse Cavalry.'"[55]

The Hoover administration's evil machinations, in true Judeo-Christian form, had "brought upon us a terrible retribution." The retribution, to a large extent, was manifested in the nation's collective health: The Four Horsemen had left in their wake paralysis, vertigo, blindness, soreness, and tiredness. A return to health depended on a twofold rejection of the Hoover administration's treatment: a rejection of its "bitter medicine" (legislation) and its bedside manner. Hope was vital to economic recovery, but Hoover had resorted "to the most plaintive diagnosis of a doctor in despair that any country has ever heard from responsible statesmen."[56] Whereas Hoover "preached" despair, Roosevelt "preached" hope, and it was this optimistic outlook that would lead the nation to the economic resurrection.

The second train trip was just as successful as the first, as attested to by Robert Barry in an essay titled, "9,000 Miles with Franklin Roosevelt." Without mentioning the candidate's disability, Barry attempted to lay to rest any notion that Roosevelt was unfit for the physical demands of the presidency. "I am willing to go a long way with Franklin D. Roosevelt on his political idealism," he began. But "as a traveling companion on a transcontinental campaign trip I want no more of him. You can have him. This President-to-be of ours isn't human. He is some kind of machine. A robot possibly. Certainly a dynamo." He continued, "If there is such a thing as 'the pace that kills' Governor Roosevelt has it copyrighted. It is all but fatal for everyone except himself. He seems actually to thrive on it. It really appears to do him good."[57] Even from across the Atlantic, the verdict of *The Times* of London was that Roosevelt's train trip had convincingly succeeded: "Hundreds of thousands have seen the figure of this lame man with the torso of an athlete, who has said little enough, but whose appearance in State after State and whose abounding vitality have made the whispers of his crippled and invalid condition barely audible."[58]

But Roosevelt was not yet through campaigning. On October 30, to a nationwide radio audience, Roosevelt avoided the extremism and hyperbole associated with a millennial economic drama; instead, he talked about life in a postdepression United States. He cast the period in terms that perhaps only a victim of traumatic illness could appreciate: "These surface indications [of depression] are bad enough in themselves, but the deep-seated, invisible injuries that this depression is causing are likely to bear tragic consequences for generations to come." Roosevelt had a privileged or internal view of the nation's future suffering, not because of a prophetic gift, but because of something far more profound, something he had himself experienced: "There are wounds that will heal, but there are scars that the sufferers will feel all the rest of their lives—scars that will affect not only them, but their families and their neighbors."[59] This statement was perhaps the closest that Roosevelt came—at least in the 1932 campaign—to a public disclosure regarding his ongoing battle with infantile paralysis. While the polio virus had left his body, its residual damage had profoundly affected him and his relationship to those around him. Thus, at an experiential level, Roosevelt, ironically, was most fit to lead; having been in a perpetual state of recovery for more than eleven years, he knew intimately and instinctually what convalescence entailed—both psychically and physically.

The final week of the campaign was a rhetorical microcosm of the larger whole, with one significant exception. Up to this point in the general election campaign, Roosevelt had avoided any talk of warfare that directly involved the people. He had indeed mentioned war, but he did so typically in the context of a personal war that he was waging against Hoover and his administration. But in his November 4 speech to the Brooklyn Academy of Music, Roosevelt broadened the metaphor for the first time since July 2 to include the people: "In simple terms I have attempted to say to the people of this country that the way out of disaster and depression is a battle to be fought by the people."[60] Roosevelt also made warfare the master metaphor in his final major campaign address—a brief speech broadcast live to the nation from New York's Madison Square Garden. The selection of the locale was not without historical irony; the site of the Democrats' darkest hours in

1924 was now home to a jubilant party and its triumphant candidate. The profound wounds opened up at that convention were symbolically healed by the only figure to emerge from it unscathed.

In many ways, the speech provided a fitting finale to Roosevelt's campaign. In other respects it appears anomalous; one typically does not declare wars and create armies at the end of a ten-month battle, especially when the metaphor of health and sickness had done much of the inventional work. Yet Roosevelt knew that the "real" battle was just beginning. Nearly everyone, including Herbert and Lou Hoover, knew that Roosevelt would be the nation's next president; as such, he was likely looking ahead to his Inaugural Address and the war that he would declare on that day. But there was another reason for the metaphorical switch as the campaign reached its final hours: a sick country would be sick no longer. The nation needed activity, energy—something to get behind. It could not fight a battle back to health from a sickbed; as such, Roosevelt declared war on a sickness that needed physical, able bodies to fight, not on the inward Hooverian battle for mental health and confidence. Part of this preparation for March 4, 1933, was to create, or to "constitute," an army, one devoid of partisan and class divisions. And Roosevelt skillfully constituted the ranks of his army by creating a discursive space for nearly all economic groups. Roosevelt proceeded to call roll:

> There is among you the man who is not bound by party lines. . . . There is among you the woman who knows that women's traditional interests— welfare, children and the home—rest on the broader basis of an economic system which assures her or her husband of a job. . . . There is among you the man in business or in trade who has heard the cry that change was a fearful thing but who, unafraid, has decided to change. . . . There is among you the man who has been brought up in the good American tradition to work hard and to save for a rainy day. . . . There is among you the man who has been brought up to believe that a livelihood could always be wrung from the soil by willing labor. . . . There is among you the man who has been able to save something from this wreck.[61]

Roosevelt's seemingly detached appeal to "the man" and "the woman" was very misleading, for he uttered the term "you" or "your" more than eighty times in just fifteen minutes. More importantly, Roosevelt's use of the second person was augmented and ultimately transcended by an inclusive rhetoric that featured more than sixty references to "we," "our," and "us." He eloquently merged the singular and the plural in his only explicit mention of war: "All of you . . . have helped shape the policies of the Democratic party in this, its war on human suffering. Your own experiences and your own fears and your own problems—all have written themselves into our program. There is something of you in all of us."[62] Thus had the metaphor of sickness and health come full circle: The nation did indeed partake of the same substance as its political leaders. But the metaphor also implied that the corporate consubstantiation worked the other way as well: There was something of Franklin Roosevelt in all of them—in sickness and in health. This point was not lost on the candidate. On the last day of his life when he would not be either president or president-elect, Roosevelt spoke to his friends and well-wishers gathered near his home in Poughkeepsie. The crippled candidate, the one who had questioned whether God had abandoned him back in the dark summer days of 1921, could now conclude: "Favor comes because for a brief moment in the great space of human change and progress some general human purpose finds in him a satisfactory embodiment. . . . I seek to be only the humble emblem of this restoration of America."[63]

And so he was. On the following day, November 8, 1932, Roosevelt won the presidency by a decisive majority, 472 electoral votes to Hoover's 59. Eleanor Roosevelt, the person largely responsible for her husband's successful convalescence and reentry into politics, understood the victory as compensation: "'I knew that in many ways it would make up for the blow that fate had dealt him when he was stricken with infantile paralysis.'"[64] The victory would also bring a temporary end to the whispering, to the doubts about his health that he had lived with for more than eleven years— with perhaps one exception. That evening, as his eldest son "Jimmy" helped put his father to bed, Roosevelt perhaps for the first time internalized the enormity of what he had been elected to do. That internalization, of course, was experienced within his own body: "'You know, Jimmy,' he said, 'All my life I have been afraid of only one thing—fire. Tonight I think I'm afraid of something else.' 'Afraid of what, Pa?' I said. 'I'm just afraid,' he said, 'that I may not have the strength to do this job. After you leave me tonight, Jimmy,' he went on, 'I am going to pray. I am going to pray that God will help me, that He will give me the strength and the guidance to do this job and to do it right. I hope that you will pray for me, too, Jimmy.'"[65]

8   Body Politics

IF JAMES "JIMMY" ROOSEVELT prayed that fateful evening of his father's win at the polls, someone seemed to answer him—and most favorably. Unless the Constitution is altered, his father will go down as the nation's only four-term president. Maybe those who knew him best were not exaggerating when they claimed that traveling, giving speeches, meeting people, and campaigning generally, truly enlivened him. When we pause to consider the physical devastation of the office on even the most physically fit presidents, Roosevelt's twelve-year tenure of leading the nation through the Great Depression and then World War II is all the more remarkable. Clearly, his health and stamina should not have been an issue leading up to and including his run for the presidency in 1932. But it was, and as we have documented, from 1921 to 1932 there was no bigger issue in Roosevelt's political life.

That issue did not die with him on April 12, 1945; it really only commenced a lengthy and rancorous debate that again centered squarely on Roosevelt's body. This time the debate involved how Americans wanted to remember the twentieth century's most important president. Should a public memorial not depict Roosevelt in his wheelchair and leg braces? Or should the nation, fifty years after his death, finally admit the secret in the most public and enduring of ways? Ultimately that debate seemed to crystallize around the age-old issue of the emperor having no clothes. But this emperor was dead. Perhaps, then, the debate was more a question of whether a nation could bring itself to admit that its former leader "had no clothes." Perhaps the nation's "manhood" was at stake, its image of itself somehow retroactively imperiled by the publicly financed visage of a badly crippled man.

The public debate over the FDR Memorial was instructive at several levels, but for us, the cultural construction of disability comes front and center. Roosevelt, after all, was not disabled by nature; his disability was not written on his body on the day that he contracted infantile paralysis. Instead, a condition must become dis-abling; it must be adjudicated in a culture for any condition to be deemed as such. And so fifty years after his death, a great many Americans still clearly viewed (and view) Roosevelt's disability as dis-abling.

At the seventy-year anniversary of his first election to the presidency, we pause to consider that had Roosevelt entertained presidential aspirations in our day, he would be laughed out of the political arena. Can we see Roosevelt slogging through the slush in his wheelchair down the streets of Nashua? How would he respond to the first town hall questioner who asked him, no, commanded him, to step back from the podium and walk—unaided? What of the Gen-X, MTV voter who, instead of querying the squire about boxers or briefs, asked about his sex life with the missus? How would a very cynical electorate react to writers like Earle Looker and doctors like E. W. Beckwith whose stated desire is to get to the truth of things? And, of course, what of the press when the candidate pulled up in a car or bus or airplane and declared, "Sorry, guys, no pictures today"? Our purported progress on the issue of disability seems nothing if not retarded when considered in the bright light of contemporary presidential electoral politics. Old politics, primarily oral politics, was what Richard Weaver might call "spacious" politics; candidates were expected to have a zone of privacy, perhaps even secrets.[1]

In considering the cultural construction of disability we would do well also to distinguish among the many types of disability, especially those that are seen as dis-abling. Roosevelt, we should note, was not the first presidential candidate to have a bodily disability. Nor was he the last. The case of Sen. Bob Dole's 1996 candidacy is particularly relevant. In her Oprah-like, prime-time walk and talk around the convention hall in San Diego, Elizabeth Dole detailed in no small degree the extent of her husband's badly damaged arm and shoulder. This damage was no disability; instead, the aspiring first wife deemed it her husband's "badge of honor." The point is clear: Being nearly mortally wounded by Nazi-fired bullets in World War II was a point of pride, a most en-abling bodily mark, a "condition" to be celebrated—and publicized. Bob Dole could also walk, a point subtly underscored by his wife's peripatetic oration.

Infantile paralysis was far from a glamorous, prime-time, culturally lauded wound; rather, it was a badly misunderstood and badly dis-abling condition—thus the attempts to hide it. Roosevelt would eventually put a new face on the disease, but doing so would take time as well as some educating. That Roosevelt never really discussed his affliction in twelve years as president speaks extensively about the stigma associated with it. His condition was thus doubly dis-abling; the material effects of his condition were both physical and cultural. The symbiosis was one that even a skilled rhetorician like Roosevelt could never completely uncouple.

Infantile paralysis, as its name would suggest, was also an emasculating disease. Laying waste to a politician's legs was, as Jim Farley aptly noted, like clipping an eagle's wings. Even before we expected our presidents to sail, throw a football, ride a horse, jog around the Mall in Washington, D.C., split firewood, and play golf, we expected them to be active, vigorous, and certainly heterosexual. That the presidency is a place for fully masculine men is attested to by a *Newsweek* magazine cover story from October, 1987. The vice-president, George H. W. Bush, is pictured skippering a boat. That image, though, is undermined by the caption, which reads, "Fighting the 'Wimp Factor.'" Why a man like Bush would have his masculinity questioned on the front of one of the nation's largest circulation weekly news magazines is vexing. Here was a man who had bravely defended his country by flying combat missions in the Pacific theater during World War II, a man who was a fine collegiate athlete (baseball) at Yale, who was an avid outdoorsman, and who had fathered six children with his wife Barbara. It seems that even our "fittest" men come under fire when the presidency is their ambition.

Infantile paralysis also raised the specter of Roosevelt's masculinity—was he man "enough" for the job? James H. MacLafferty, like many, clearly felt that a Roosevelt candidacy and campaign would be a "lady-like" affair. There were even relatives who wondered about his masculinity, as a revealing diary entry of cousin Margaret "Daisy" Suckley implies. In an entry dated August 7, 1933, Daisy made this private declaration about Franklin Roosevelt: "'The President is a *MAN*—mentally, physically & spiritually—What more can I say?'"[2] Daisy, Roosevelt's closest companion at the close of his life, could have said a great deal more. Why the need for emphasis? How had Roosevelt "proven" his manliness? Did she have doubts prior to him becoming president? Physically speaking, masculinity was clearly a performance, and Roosevelt had obviously persuaded many that he was indeed physically fit for the office. As we have documented, the performance utilized both visual and verbal means. Perfecting the appearance that he could walk, even if it was only a few feet, was compelling proof—perhaps then irrefutable—that Roosevelt was no invalid. He could control his own body, or so his audiences were led to believe. Moreover, Roosevelt displayed great vigor and courage by waging such active campaigns. Daily, he was putting his body at great risk, a "body-in-stress," to borrow from Carroll C. Arnold. And daily, he was proving to all those around him that he had mastered his own body. With each successful public appearance, the Roosevelt campaign could add one more evidentiary piece to the puzzle, which they were not shy about using in the campaign materials.

Roosevelt was also lucky. One of the hallmarks of his political skill was an impeccable sense of timing. If he could control a situation, drama was always on his side. But in the summer and fall of 1932, Roosevelt had little if any control over how the country had come to know and understand the Great Depression. Roosevelt loved nicknames, and he reserved one of his favorites for himself, "Dr. New Deal." It was a moniker most appropriate to the times. In the presidential campaign of 1936, he would describe the patient in eerily familiar terms: "But I know how sick they were. I have their fever charts. I know how the knees of all our rugged individuals were trembling four years ago and how their hearts fluttered. They came to Washington in great numbers. Washington did not look like a dangerous bureaucracy," recalled the president. "Oh no! It looked like an emergency hospital. All of the distinguished patients wanted two things—a quick hypodermic to end the pain and a course of treatment to cure the disease. They wanted them in a hurry; we gave them both." Dr. Roosevelt could now conclude, "And now most of the patients seem to be doing very nicely. Some of them are even well enough to throw their crutches at the doctor."[3]

In the 1920s Roosevelt frequently noted in his correspondence that he would soon throw away his crutches. And he did. By the fall of 1926 he was "walking" only with the aid of a cane and a hefty arm. In 1936, though, Roosevelt was the attending physician and many of his patients had come, in four years, to the point where they too could throw away their crutches. So by rhetorical default, Roosevelt inherited a most efficacious metaphor, one that contributed greatly to an identification between himself and his audience. Garry Wills, among others, notes the link between Roosevelt's illness and his response to the Great Depression: "He knew that the soul needed healing first, and the confidence he had instilled in the patients of Warm Springs was the most measurable gift Roosevelt gave to the nation during the Depression." Furthermore, Roosevelt "understood the importance of psychology—that people have to have the courage to keep seeking a cure, no matter what the cure is. America had lost its will to recover, and Roosevelt was certain that regaining it was the first order of business."[4]

But Roosevelt went one step further. Whether consciously or not, Roosevelt frequently employed metaphors of the body that proved useful for his aspirations. He was the candidate who was "running," "standing," "going up and down," "looking ahead," and getting a "firm footing." These words were not the vernacular of a disabled man but rather of a fit, active, vigorous, and healthy man. Roosevelt also capitalized on Hoover's rhetorical mistakes. He perhaps sensed that an inward and individual emphasis on mental confidence was, in the midst of grave economic events, terribly debilitating. How could people have hope when they were wondering about the next meal? More than most, Roosevelt seemed instinctively to understand the healing powers of a good attitude coupled with a goal to work toward. In 1921, Uncle Fred had helped to provide Franklin with that attitude and frame of mind. Louis Howe and Eleanor Roosevelt provided the aim. By 1932 Americans had suffered enough that they now needed to do something other than hope for the best; thus, in November of that year the candidate roused and rallied Americans to join him in a march on the road to recovery. Four months later he would prescribe a memorable medicine in the midst of the nation's worst banking crisis. Like their healer, the sick and paralyzed would rise again—and walk.

NOTES

Chapter 1

1. "Remarks by the President at the Dedication Ceremony of the Franklin Delano Roosevelt Memorial," West Potomac Park, Washington, D.C., May 2, 1997, p. 5. Located online at <www.hatemonitor.org/pres_activity/clinton/ franklin_roosevelt.html> (Center for the State of Hate and Extremism, California State University, San Bernardino).

2. Ibid., p. 6.

3. "Transcript: Clinton Speaks at FDR Statue Unveiling," January 10, 2001. Located online at <http://usembassy.state.gov/tokyo/wwwhs082.html> (Public Affairs Section of the U.S. Embassy, Japan).

4. Homer, *The Iliad,* trans. Robert Fagles (New York: Viking, 1997), p. 106.

5. Ibid.

6. Ibid., p. 107.

7. Ibid., p. 108.

8. For a similar view of disability see, David T. Mitchell and Sharon L. Snyder, "Introduction: Disability Studies and the Double Bind of Representation," in *The Body and Physical Difference: Discourses of Disability,* ed. Mitchell and Snyder (Ann Arbor: University of Michigan Press, 1998), pp. 1–31; Helen Meekosha, "Body Battles: Bodies, Gender and Disability," in *The Disability Reader,* ed. Tom Shakespeare (London: Cassell, 1998), p. 167; Simi Linton, *Claiming Disability: Knowledge and Identity* (New York: New York University Press, 1998), p. 2; Mary Klages, *Woeful Afflictions: Disability and Sentimentality in Victorian America* (Philadelphia: University of Pennsylvania Press, 1999), pp. 2, 10; Mairian Corker and Sally French, "Reclaiming Discourse in Disability Studies," in *Disability Discourse,* ed. Corker and French (Buckingham, England: Open Press University, 1999), pp. 1–11; and Lennard J. Davis, introduction to *The Disability Studies Reader,* ed. Davis (New York: Routledge, 1997), p. 3.

9. See Roderick P. Hart, *The Sound of Leadership: Presidential Communication in the Modern Age* (Chicago: University of Chicago Press, 1987); Lloyd Bitzer, "The Rhetorical Situation," *Philosophy & Rhetoric* 1 (1968): 5; Karlyn Kohrs Campbell and Kathleen Hall Jamieson, *Deeds Done in Words: Presidential Rhetoric and the Genres of Governance* (Chicago: University of Chicago Press, 1990); Michel Foucault, *The Archaeology of Knowledge and the Discourse on Language,* trans. A. M. Sheridan Smith (New York: Pantheon, 1972); Carole Blair, "Contemporary U.S. Memorial Sites as Exemplars of Rhetorical Materiality," in *Rhetorical Bodies,* ed. Jack Selzer and Sharon Crowley (Madison: University of Wisconsin Press, 1999), p. 30; Kenneth Burke, *Language as Symbolic Action* (Berkeley: University of California Press, 1968).

10.   Carroll C. Arnold, "Oral Rhetoric, Rhetoric, and Literature," *Philosophy & Rhetoric* 1 (1968): 195. Similarly, Dorinda Outram states that "words do not give up their full meaning without an account of the physical behavior which accompanies them" (*The Body and the French Revolution: Sex, Class, and Political Culture* [New Haven: Yale University Press, 1989], p. 34).

11.   Arnold, "Oral Rhetoric," pp. 197, 206.

12.   Anne Norton, *Republic of Signs: Liberal Theory and American Popular Culture* (Chicago: University of Chicago Press, 1993), p. 120.

13.   Michael S. Kimmel, "Invisible Masculinity," *Society* 30 (1993): 28.

14.   R. W. Connell, *Masculinities* (Berkeley: University of California Press, 1995), p. 54.

15.   Theo Lippman, Jr., *The Squire of Warm Springs: F.D.R. in Georgia, 1924–1945* (Chicago: Playboy Press, 1977), p. 65.

16.   Mitchell and Snyder, "Introduction: Disability Studies and the Double Bind," p. 1; Karen Hirsch, "Culture and Disability: The Role of Oral History," *Oral History Review* 22 (1995): 3.

17.   Jack Selzer, "Habeas Corpus: An Introduction," in *Rhetorical Bodies,* ed. Selzer and Sharon Crowley (Madison: University of Wisconsin Press, 1999), p. 4.

18.   Selzer, "Habeas Corpus: An Introduction," pp. 3–15; Blair, "Contemporary U.S. Memorial Sites," pp. 18–20; Brenda Jo Brueggemann and James A. Fredal, "Studying Disability Rhetorically," in *Disability Discourse,* ed. Mairian Corker and Sally French (Buckingham, England: Open University Press, 1999), pp. 129–35; and James C. Wilson and Cynthia Lewiecki-Wilson, "Disability, Rhetoric, and the Body," in *Embodied Rhetorics: Disability in Language and Culture,* ed. Wilson and Lewiecki-Wilson (Carbondale: Southern Illinois University Press, 2001), pp. 1–24.

19.   FDR, "Address at Oglethorpe University, May 22, 1932," in Franklin D. Roosevelt, *The Public Papers and Addresses of Franklin D. Roosevelt,* comp. Samuel I. Rosenman (New York: Random House, 1938), 1:646.

20.   Geoffrey C. Ward, *A First-Class Temperament: The Emergence of Franklin Roosevelt* (New York: Harper & Row, 1989), p. 750. See also Kenneth R. Crispell and Carlos F. Gomez, *Hidden Illness in the White House* (Durham, N.C.: Duke University Press, 1988).

21.   Hugh Gregory Gallagher, *FDR's Splendid Deception* (New York: Dodd, Mead, 1985); Richard Thayer Goldberg, *The Making of Franklin D. Roosevelt: Triumph over Disability* (Cambridge, Mass: Abt, 1981); Jean Gould, *A Good Fight: The Story of F.D.R.'s Conquest of Polio* (New York: Dodd, Mead, 1960); Frank Freidel, *Franklin D. Roosevelt: The Ordeal* (Boston: Little, Brown, 1954); and Ward, *A First-Class Temperament.*

22.   See George C. Edwards III, "Presidential Rhetoric: What Difference Does It Make?" *Beyond the Rhetorical Presidency,* ed. Martin J. Medhurst (College Station: Texas A&M University Press, 1996), pp. 199–217.

Chapter 2

1.   Our account of Roosevelt's harrowing month at Campobello is based largely on family correspondence that survives. For the most detailed account of the period, see Ward, *A First-Class Temperament,* pp. 576–99. While we do borrow from Ward, there are some minor disagreements regarding dates. To adjudicate such disagreements, we have opted to use the dates mentioned in the family's correspondence.

2.   "Mrs. F. D. R. Interview, Session 4," Polio, Vertical File, FDR Papers, Franklin D. Roosevelt Presidential Library, Hyde Park, N.Y. (hereafter cited as FRPL).

3.   Quoted in Ward, *A First-Class Temperament,* p. 584.

4.   "Mrs. F. D. R. Interview, Session 4."

5.   Eleanor Roosevelt to "Rosy" Roosevelt, Aug. 14, 1921, Family, Business, and Personal Papers, Box 23, FDR Papers, FRPL.

6.   Ibid.

7.   Louis Howe to Townsend, Aug. 18, 1921, Family, Business, and Personal Papers, Box 23, FDR Papers, FRPL.

8.   Eleanor Roosevelt to "Rosy" Roosevelt, Aug. 18, 1921, Family, Business, and Personal Papers, Box 23, FDR Papers, FRPL.

9.   Frederick Delano to Eleanor Roosevelt, Aug. 20, 1921, Family, Business, and Personal Papers, Box 23, FDR Papers, FRPL.

10.   Ibid.

11.   Quoted in Gould, *A Good Fight,* p. 24.

12.   Naomi Rogers, *Dirt and Disease: Polio before FDR* (New Brunswick, N.J.: Rutgers University Press, 1992), p. 21.

13.   Ibid., p. 29.

14.   Gallagher, *FDR's Splendid Deception,* p. 21. See also Ward, *A First-Class Temperament,* p. 618; and Goldberg, *The Making of Franklin D. Roosevelt,* pp. 32–33.

15.   See, for example, E. Anthony Rotundo, "Body and Soul: Changing Ideals of American Middle-Class Manhood, 1770–1920," *Journal of Social History* 16 (1983): 23–38; and Michael S. Kimmel, "Consuming Manhood: The Feminization of American Culture and the Recreation of the Male Body, 1832–1920," *Michigan Quarterly Review* 33 (1994): 7–33.

16.   Eleanor Roosevelt to "Rosy" Roosevelt, Aug. 23, 1921, Family, Business, and Personal Papers, Box 23, FDR Papers, FRPL.

17.   "Mrs. F. D. R. Interview, Session 4."

18.   Frederick Delano to Eleanor Roosevelt, Aug. 28, 1921, Family, Business, and Personal Papers, Box 23, FDR Papers, FRPL.

19.   Ibid.

20.   "Franklin D. Roosevelt Ill," *New York Times,* Aug. 27, 1921, p. 9.

21.   Eleanor Roosevelt to "Rosy" Roosevelt, Aug. 14, 1921.

22.   Ibid.

23.   Quoted in Sara Roosevelt to Frederic Delano, Sept. 2, 1921, Family, Business, and Personal Papers, Box 23, FDR Papers, FRPL.

24.   Ibid.

25.   Eleanor Roosevelt to Dr. William Keen, Aug. 29, 1921, Family, Business, and Personal Papers, Box 23, FDR Papers, FRPL.

26.   Quoted in Ward, *A First-Class Temperament,* p. 592.

27.   "Franklin D. Roosevelt Better," *New York Times,* Aug. 29, 1921, p. 11.

28.   "Franklin D. Roosevelt Improving," *New York Times,* Sept. 10, 1921, p. 4.

29.   Ward, *A First-Class Temperament,* p. 608.

30.   Frederic Delano to Franklin Roosevelt, Sept. 4, 1921, Family, Business, and Personal Papers, Box 23, FDR Papers, FRPL.

31.   Anna Roosevelt, "The Real Truth about FDR's Health," Box 52, Anna Roosevelt Halsted Papers, FRPL.

32.   Quoted in Ward, *A First-Class Temperament,* p. 599.

33.   Quoted in ibid., p. 601.

34.   James "Rosy" Roosevelt to Franklin Roosevelt, Sept. 8, 1921, Condolence Letters to FDR, Family and Personal Correspondence, Box 1, Eleanor Roosevelt Papers, FRPL.

35.   William Gibbs McAdoo to Franklin Roosevelt, Sept. 16, 1921, Condolence Letters to FDR, Family and Personal Correspondence, Box 1, Eleanor Roosevelt Papers, FRPL.

36.   Quoted in Ward, *A First-Class Temperament,* p. 603.

37.   "F. D. Roosevelt Ill of Poliomyelitis," *New York Times,* Sept. 16, 1921, p. 1.

38.   Freidel, *Franklin D. Roosevelt: The Ordeal,* p. 101.

39.   Quoted in John Gunther, *Roosevelt in Retrospect: A Profile in History* (New York: Harper, 1950), p. 225.

40.   Dr. Robert Lovett to Dr. E. H. Bennett, Sept. 2, 1921, Family, Business, and Personal Papers, Box 23, FDR Papers, FRPL.

41.   Eleanor Roosevelt to Dr. William Keen, Sept. 26, 1921, Family, Business, and Personal Papers, Box 23, FDR Papers, FRPL.

42.   Quoted in Gunther, *Roosevelt in Retrospect,* pp. 225–26.

43.   Quoted in ibid., p. 226.

44.   Lily Norton to Helen Whidden, Nov. 14, 1921, Reminiscences of FDR and ER by Contemporaries, 1893–1945, Box 1, FDR Papers, FRPL.

Chapter 3

1.   Eleanor Roosevelt to Dr. William Keen, Nov. 13, 1921, Family, Business, and Personal Papers, Box 23, FDR Papers, FRPL.

2.   Franklin Roosevelt to Dr. William Keen, June 19, 1922, Miscellaneous Documents, Small Collection, Box 1, FDR Papers, FRPL.

3.   Franklin Roosevelt to George Draper, Aug. 10, 1922, Family, Business, and Personal Papers, Box 23, FDR Papers, FRPL.

4.   Franklin Roosevelt to Dr. William Keen, Aug. 10, 1922, Miscellaneous Documents, Small Collection, Box 1, FDR Papers, FRPL.

5.   Franklin Roosevelt to Paul Hasbrouck, Oct. 17, 1923, Family, Business, and Personal Papers, Box 23, FDR Papers, FRPL.

6.   Thos. F. Durning to Louis Howe, Dec. 29, 1923, Box 19, Louis McHenry Howe Papers, FRPL.

7.   Franklin Roosevelt to the Democratic National Committee (undated, though labeled as 1921), Family, Business, and Personal Papers, Box 41, FDR Papers, FRPL.

8.   Freidel, *Franklin D. Roosevelt: The Ordeal,* p. 176.

9.   Kenneth S. Davis, *Invincible Summer: An Intimate Portrait of the Roosevelts Based on the Recollections of Marion Dickerman* (New York: Atheneum, 1974), p. 2.

10.   Quoted in Gunther, *Roosevelt in Retrospect,* p. 246.

11.   The text that Roosevelt wrote was not delivered; see Davis, *Invincible Summer,* p. 29.

12.   FDR, "Nominating Alfred E. Smith, 1924," Speech Files, Oct. 21, 1920–Sept. 27, 1926, FDR Papers, FRPL.

13.   Ibid., pp. 15, 17.

14.   "F. D. Roosevelt Gets Ovation," *Washington Star,* June 26, 1924, clipping in Scrapbook, Campaign of 1924, Box 24, FDR Papers, FRPL.

15. See *Eagle News,* July 2, 1924, clipping in Scrapbook, Campaign of 1924, Box 24, FDR Papers, FRPL.

16. "F. D. Roosevelt Looms Up as Possible Candidate," *Evening Star,* July 1, 1924, clipping in Scrapbook, Campaign of 1924, Box 24, FDR Papers, FRPL.

17. Louis Riley to Franklin D. Roosevelt, June 27, 1924, Scrapbook, Campaign of 1924, Box 14, FDR Papers, FRPL.

18. *Louisville Courier-Journal,* July, 1924, clipping in Scrapbook, Campaign of 1924, Box 15, FDR Papers, FRPL.

19. *New York Herald Tribune,* June 28, 1924, p. 6.

20. Kyle D. Palmer, "Ku Klux Hood and Gown Foil Democratic Craft," *Los Angeles Times,* June 27, 1924, p. 6.

21. Robert M. Lee, "Nothing But Smith as Gentlemen from Bowery Pack Gallery, *Los Angeles Times,* June 27, 1924, p. 3.

22. Freidel, *Franklin D. Roosevelt: The Ordeal,* p. 180.

23. Ibid.

24. "FDR Returned from Warm Springs," *Washington Star,* Aug. 9, 1924, clipping in Scrapbook, Campaign of 1924, Box 24, FDR Papers, FRPL.

25. *New York Evening Post,* Oct. 18, 1924, clipping in Scrapbook, Campaign of 1924, Box 24, FDR Papers, FRPL.

26. *Washington Star,* Oct. 29, 1924, clipping in Scrapbook, Campaign of 1924, Box 24, FDR Papers, FRPL.

27. Unidentified clipping in Scrapbook, Campaign of 1924, Box 14, FDR Papers, FRPL.

28. Quoted in Freidel, *Franklin D. Roosevelt: The Ordeal,* p. 184.

29. Jim Farley, "Embarkation," Box 82, Ernest Cuneo Papers, FRPL.

30. Frank W. Sterling to Franklin D. Roosevelt, July 28, 1924, Scrapbook, Campaign of 1924, Box 14, FDR Papers, FRPL.

31. Jerry B. Sullivan to Franklin D. Roosevelt, June 27, 1924, Scrapbook, Campaign of 1924, Box 14, FDR Papers, FRPL.

32. J. Frederic Tams to Franklin D. Roosevelt, June 27, 1924, Scrapbook, Campaign of 1924, Box 14, FDR Papers, FRPL.

33. Jedediah Tingle to Franklin D. Roosevelt, Aug. 5, 1924, Scrapbook, Campaign of 1924, Box 14, FDR Papers, FRPL.

34. Joseph F. Valentine to Franklin D. Roosevelt, June 30, 1924, Scrapbook, Campaign of 1924, Box 14, FDR Papers, FRPL.

35. Franklin D. Roosevelt to Mr. Valentine, Aug. 14, 1924, Scrapbook, Campaign of 1924, Box 14, FDR Papers, FRPL.

36. Francis M. Wilson to Franklin D. Roosevelt, June 26, 1924, Scrapbook, Campaign of 1924, Box 14, FDR Papers, FRPL.

37. James Wilson to Franklin D. Roosevelt, July 10, 1924, Scrapbook, Campaign of 1924, Box 14, FDR Papers, FRPL.

38. Arthur Van Rensselaer to Franklin D. Roosevelt, July 21, 1924, Scrapbook, Campaign of 1924, Box 14, FDR Papers, FRPL.

39. Franklin D. Roosevelt to Mr. Van Rensselaer, July 29, 1924, Scrapbook, Campaign of 1924, Box 14, FDR Papers, FRPL.

40. Franklin D. Roosevelt to Mrs. Walther, July 23, 1924, Scrapbook, Campaign of 1924, Box 14, FDR Papers, FRPL.

41. Franklin D. Roosevelt to Professor Wells, July 24, 1924, Scrapbook, Campaign of 1924, Box 14, FDR Papers, FRPL.

42. Irving Washburn to Franklin D. Roosevelt, July 11, 1924, Scrapbook, Campaign of 1924, Box 14, FDR Papers, FRPL.

43. Franklin D. Roosevelt to Mr. Washburn, July 24, 1924, Scrapbook, Campaign of 1924, Box 14, FDR Papers, FRPL.

44. Franklin Roosevelt to S. R. Betron, Sept. 4, 1924, Family, Business, and Personal Papers, Box 23, FDR Papers, FRPL.

45. Quoted in Elliott Roosevelt, ed., *F.D.R.: His Personal Letters,* vol. 2, *1905–1928* (New York: Duell, Sloan and Pearce, 1950), p. 568.

46. Franklin Roosevelt to Paul Hasbrouck, Jan. 12, 1925, Family, Business, and Personal Papers, Box 23, FDR Papers, FRPL.

47. Quoted in Gallagher, *FDR's Splendid Deception,* pp. 37–38.

48. Franklin Roosevelt to Dr. George Draper, Sept. 30, 1925, Family, Business, and Personal Papers, Box 23, FDR Papers, FRPL.

49. Anna Roosevelt to Eleanor Roosevelt, April, 1926, File 7, Box 59, Halsted Papers, FRPL.

50. Quoted in Freidel, *Franklin D. Roosevelt: The Ordeal,* p. 199.

51. Freidel, *Franklin D. Roosevelt: The Ordeal,* p. 214.

52. FDR, Editorial, *Daily Telegraph (Macon, Ga.),* Apr. 24, 1925, Family, Business, and Personal File, Box 41, FDR Papers, FRPL.

53. Freidel, *Franklin D. Roosevelt: The Ordeal,* p. 215.

54. Quoted in Freidel, *Franklin D. Roosevelt: The Ordeal,* p. 216.

55. Louis Howe to Franklin Roosevelt, undated, Box 19, Howe Papers, FRPL.

56. Franklin Roosevelt to Dr. William Keen, Aug. 24, 1926, Miscellaneous Documents, Small Collection, Box 1, FDR Papers, FRPL.

57. FDR, "Whither Bound?" p. 1, May 18, 1926, Family, Business, and Personal Papers, Writing and Statement File, Box 41, FDR Papers, FRPL.

58. Ibid., p. 2.

59. Ibid., p. 6.

60. Ibid., p. 13.

61. Ibid., p. 15.

62. Freidel, *Franklin D. Roosevelt: The Ordeal,* p. 227.

63. "An Active Sick Man," *Boston News Bureau,* June 6, 1927, pp. 35–36, clipping in Family, Business, and Personal Papers, Box 23, FDR Papers, FRPL.

64. "Roosevelt to Aid Stricken," unidentified clipping, Paul D. Hasbrouck File, Box 1, FDR Papers, FRPL.

65. Gunther, *Roosevelt in Retrospect,* p. 234.

Chapter 4

1. Davis, *Invincible Summer,* p. 80.

2. Richard V. Oulahan, "Governor Smith Is Put in Nomination Amid Wild Cheers," *New York Times,* June 28, 1928, p. 1.

3. Quoted in Gunther, *Roosevelt in Retrospect,* p. 250.

4. Freidel, *Franklin D. Roosevelt: The Ordeal,* p. 251.

5. Louis Howe, telegram to Franklin Roosevelt, Sept. 25, 1928, File 3, Box 40, Howe Papers, FRPL.

6. Louis Howe, telegram to Franklin Roosevelt, Sept. 26, 1928, File 3, Box 40, Howe Papers, FRPL.

7. Louis Howe, telegram to Franklin Roosevelt, Sept. 26, 1928, File 3, Box 40, Howe Papers, FRPL.

8. Louis Howe, telegram to Franklin Roosevelt, Sept. 26, 1928, 6:41 P.M., File 3, Box 40, Howe Papers, FRPL.

9. Louis Howe, telegram to Franklin Roosevelt, Sept. 28, 1928, File 3, Box 40, Howe Papers, FRPL.

10. Louis Howe, telegram to Franklin Roosevelt, Oct. 1, 1928, File 3, Box 40, Howe Papers, FRPL.

11. Quoted in "Health Forbids Acceptance, Is Roosevelt Wire," *Elmira (New York) Advertiser,* Oct. 2, 1928, p. 1.

12. "Roosevelt Accepts Nomination," *Elmira (New York) Advertiser,* Oct. 3, 1928, p. 1.

13. Freidel, *Franklin D. Roosevelt: The Ordeal,* p. 257.

14. "An Unfair Sacrifice," *New York Herald Tribune,* Oct. 3, 1928, p. 26.

15. Quoted in Freidel, *Franklin D. Roosevelt: The Ordeal,* p. 258.

16. Freidel, *Franklin D. Roosevelt: The Ordeal,* p. 259.

17. Interview with newspaper reporters, Oct. 9, 1928, Family, Business, and Personal Papers, Box 42, FDR Papers, FRPL.

18. Roosevelt's remarks quoted in the *New York Herald Tribune,* Oct. 9, 1928, and quoted in Freidel, *Franklin D. Roosevelt: The Ordeal,* p. 260.

19. "The Facts of the State Campaign," File 8, Box 67, Halsted Papers, FRPL.

20. "Extemporaneous Campaign Address, Binghamton, N.Y., October 17, 1928," in FDR, *The Public Papers and Addresses of Franklin D. Roosevelt,* 1:17.

21. Ibid.

22. FDR, Speech in Salamanca, N.Y., Oct. 19, 1928, Public Papers File: Speech File, Oct. 19, 1928–Apr. 3, 1929, Container 6, FDR Papers, FRPL.

23. "Speech in Jamestown, N.Y., Oct. 19, 1928," in FDR, *The Public Papers and Addresses of Franklin D. Roosevelt,* 1:61.

24. Speech in Wellsville, N.Y., Oct. 19, 1928, Public Papers File: Speech File, Oct. 19, 1928–Apr. 3, 1929, Container 6, FDR Papers, FRPL.

25. "Campaign Address, Buffalo, N.Y., October 20, 1928," in FDR, *The Public Papers and Addresses of Franklin D. Roosevelt,* 1:37.

26. "Fine Character of Roosevelt Wins Support," *Times of Batavia (New York),* Oct. 20, 1928, p. 1.

27. Newspaper Interview at Hotel Lafayette, Oct. 21, 1928, Family, Business, and Personal Papers, Box 42, FDR Papers, FRPL.

28. "Campaign Address, Rochester, N.Y., October 22, 1928," in FDR, *The Public Papers and Addresses of Franklin D. Roosevelt,* 1:40.

29. Ibid., 1:41.

30. *Daily Messenger (Canandaigua, N.Y.),* Oct. 22, 1928, p. 1.

31. "Franklin Roosevelt Speaks Here," *Daily Messenger (Canandaigua, N.Y.),* Oct. 23, 1928, p. 1.

32. "Big Welcome Planned for Roosevelt," *Syracuse Journal,* Oct. 23, 1928, p. 2.

33. "Rum Not State Issue, Says Roosevelt," *Syracuse Journal,* Oct. 24, 1928, p. 2.

34. FDR, Speech in Utica, N.Y., Oct. 25, 1928, Public Papers File: Speech Files, Oct. 19, 1928–Apr. 3, 1929, Box 6, FDR Papers, FRPL.

35. "Nominee of Party Stops at Herkimer," *Utica (New York) Observer-Dispatch,* Oct. 26, 1928, p. 1.

36. Quoted in Earle Looker, *This Man Roosevelt* (New York: Brewer, Warren & Putnam, 1932), p. 149.

37. "Campaign Address, Troy, N.Y., October 26, 1928," in FDR, *The Public Papers and Addresses of Franklin D. Roosevelt,* 1:53–54.

38. "Franklin D. Roosevelt Democratic Choice," *Times of Batavia (New York),* Nov. 3, 1928, p. 6.

39. Alfred B. Rollins, *Roosevelt and Howe* (New York: Knopf, 1962), p. 236.

40. Freidel, *Franklin D. Roosevelt: The Ordeal,* p. 267.

41. FDR, "Reveals to Voters about His Health," undelivered speech text, Public Papers File: Speech Files, Oct. 19, 1928–Apr. 3, 1929, Box 6, FDR Papers, FRPL.

42. Ibid.

43. Ibid.

44. FDR, Speech at the Academy of Music, Brooklyn, N.Y., Nov. 2, 1928, Public Papers File: Speech Files, Oct. 19, 1928–Apr. 3, 1929, Box 6, FDR Papers, FRPL.

45. "A Flattering Campaign," *New York Times,* Oct. 17, 1928, p. 28.

46. Charles Ritz to Franklin Roosevelt, Dec. 2, 1928, Family, Business, and Personal Papers, Box 23, FDR Papers, FRPL.

47. Jim Farley, "Roosevelt and I," Box 82, Cuneo Papers, FRPL.

48. "The First Inaugural Address as Governor, January 1, 1929," in FDR, *The Public Papers and Addresses of Franklin D. Roosevelt,* 1:76.

49. Ibid.

50. Hubbard quoted in *New York Times,* Jan. 2, 1929, quoted in Frank Freidel, *Franklin D. Roosevelt: The Triumph* (Boston: Little, Brown, 1956), p. 28.

51. Quoted in Frances Perkins, *The Roosevelt I Knew* (New York: Viking, 1946), p. 52.

52. Quoted in *New York Times,* Nov. 12, 1928, quoted in Freidel, *Franklin D. Roosevelt: The Triumph,* p. 9.

53. Quoted in *New York Times,* Jan. 18, 1929, quoted in Freidel, *Franklin D. Roosevelt: The Triumph,* p. 31.

54. Quoted in Freidel, *Franklin D. Roosevelt: The Triumph,* pp. 53–54, 68.

55. Quoted in *New York Times,* Apr. 27, 1930, quoted in Freidel, *Franklin D. Roosevelt: The Triumph,* pp. 136–37.

56. "The Candidate Accepts the Renomination for the Governorship, New York City, October 3, 1930," in FDR, *The Public Papers and Addresses of Franklin D. Roosevelt,* 1:399.

57. Ibid., 1:403.

58. "Newspaper Interview on Governor Roosevelt Accepting Delivery of $500,000 Life Insurance Policy in Favor of Georgia Warm Springs Foundation," Albany, N.Y., Oct. 18, 1930, Family, Business, and Personal Papers, Box 42, FDR Papers, FRPL.

59. Ibid., pp. 1, 2.

60. Ibid., pp. 4, 5.

61. "Campaign Address, Buffalo, N.Y., October 20, 1930," in FDR, *The Public Papers and Addresses of Franklin D. Roosevelt,* 1:406.

62. Ibid., 1:407.

63. Ibid., 1:409–12.

64. "Campaign Address, Rochester, N.Y., October 21, 1930," in FDR, *The Public Papers and Addresses of Franklin D. Roosevelt,* 1:418.

65. "Campaign Address, Syracuse, N.Y., October 22, 1930," in FDR, *The Public Papers and Addresses of Franklin D. Roosevelt,* 1:423.

66. Freidel, *Franklin D. Roosevelt: The Triumph,* p. 166.

67. Rollins, *Roosevelt and Howe,* p. 242.

68. Franklin D. Roosevelt, memo to Louis Howe, May 15, 1930, Papers as Governor, Howe File 1930, FDR Papers, FRPL.

69. Guernsey Cross to the *Newark Call,* Feb. 19, 1930, Papers as Governor, Series 1, Newa-Neup, FDR Papers, FRPL.

70. Franklin D. Roosevelt to the editor of the *Danville (Virginia) Register,* Dec. 18, 1930, Papers as Governor, Series 1, Newa-Neup, FDR Papers, FRPL.

71. *New Orleans Morning Tribune,* Mar. 2, 1931, clipping in Papers as Governor, Series 1, Newspaper Attacks on Governor, FDR Papers, FRPL.

72. Franklin D. Roosevelt to the editor of the *New Orleans Morning Tribune,* undated, Papers as Governor, Series 1, Newspaper Attacks on Governor, FDR Papers, FRPL.

73. Guernsey Cross to the *New Orleans Morning Tribune,* undated, Papers as Governor, Series 1, Newspaper Attacks on Governor, FDR Papers, FRPL.

Chapter 5

1. Franklin Roosevelt to Hamilton Mills, May 4, 1931, quoted in Freidel, *Franklin D. Roosevelt: The Triumph,* p. 210.

2. W. M. Odell to [James J. Mahoney], Oct. 1, 1930, DNC 1932, FRPL; quoted in Freidel, *Franklin D. Roosevelt: The Triumph,* p. 157.

3. Quoted in "Prohibition," *Time,* Apr. 27, 1931, p. 18.

4. Rollins, *Roosevelt and Howe,* p. 313.

5. Gallagher, *FDR's Splendid Deception,* p. 84.

6. Freidel, *Franklin D. Roosevelt: The Triumph,* p. 211.

7. Earle Looker to Eleanor Roosevelt, Dec. 16, 1930, Governorship Papers, Series 1, Earle Looker, FDR Papers, FRPL.

8. Freidel, *Franklin D. Roosevelt: The Triumph,* p. 211.

9. Jim Farley to Louis Howe, July 17, 1931, Box 25, Howe Papers, FRPL; see also Ward, *A First-Class Temperament,* p. 138.

10. Earle Looker to Franklin D. Roosevelt, July 16, 1931, Governorship Papers, Series 1, Earle Looker, FDR Papers, FRPL.

11. Earle Looker, "Is Franklin D. Roosevelt Physically Fit to Be President?" *Liberty Magazine,* July 25, 1931, pp. 6–10.

12. Farley, "Embarkation," Box 82, Cuneo Papers, FRPL.

13. *Springfield (Massachusetts) Republican,* July 18, 1931, clipping in Governorship Papers, Series 1, Earle Looker, FDR Papers, FRPL.

14.   Earle Looker to Franklin D. Roosevelt, July 20, 1931, Governorship Papers, Series 1, Earle Looker, FDR Papers, FRPL.

15.   Earle Looker to Franklin D. Roosevelt, Aug. 12, 1931, Governorship Papers, Series 1, Earle Looker, FDR Papers, FRPL.

16.   Earle Looker to Franklin D. Roosevelt, Aug. 26, 1931, Governorship Papers, Series 1, Earle Looker, FDR Papers, FRPL.

17.   Earle Looker to Franklin D. Roosevelt, Sept. 5, 1931, Governorship Papers, Series 1, Earle Looker, FDR Papers, FRPL.

18.   An outline of the chapters in Looker's *This Man Roosevelt* is filed in Memorial Foundation, Series 1, Box 23, FDR Papers, FRPL.

19.   Looker, *This Man Roosevelt*, p. 1.

20.   Ibid., p. 118.

21.   Ibid., p. 122.

22.   Ibid., p. 133.

23.   Ibid., pp. 134–35.

24.   Ibid., p. 135.

25.   Ibid., p. 136.

26.   Ibid., p. 137.

27.   Ibid., p. 140.

28.   Ibid., p. 146.

29.   Ibid., p. 147.

30.   Ibid.; Perkins, *The Roosevelt I Knew,* pp. 44–45.

31.   Looker, *This Man Roosevelt,* p. 148.

32.   Ibid., pp. 144, 155, 156, 158.

33.   Franklin D. Roosevelt to Earle Looker, Nov. 17, 1932, Governorship Papers, Series 1, Box 50, FDR Papers, FRPL.

34.   Earle Looker to Franklin D. Roosevelt, Nov. 13, 1933, President's Secretary File, Looker-Joseph folder, Box 142, FDR Papers, FRPL.

35.   Franklin D. Roosevelt to Earle Looker, Nov. 21, 1933, President's Secretary File, Looker-Joseph folder, Box 142, FDR Papers, FRPL.

Chapter 6

1.   "Political Notes," *Time,* June 15, 1931, p. 17.

2.   Raymond Moley to Nell Moley, Apr. 12, 1932, File 43, Box 38, Raymond Moley Papers, Hoover Institution on War, Revolution and Peace, Stanford, Calif. (hereafter cited as HIWRP).

3.   "The 'Forgotten Man' Speech, Radio Address, Albany, N.Y., April 7, 1932," in FDR, *The Public Papers and Addresses of Franklin D. Roosevelt,* 1:624.

4.   Ibid., 1:625.

5.   Ibid., 1:624.

6.   Ibid., 1:625, 627.

7.   Rexford G. Tugwell, *The Brains Trust* (New York: Viking, 1968), p. 50.

8.   "'A Concert of Action, Based on a Fair and Just Concert of Interests,' Address at Jefferson Day Dinner, St. Paul, Minn., April 18, 1932," in FDR, *The Public Papers and Addresses of Franklin D. Roosevelt,* 1:629.

9.   Ibid., 1:631.

10.   Ibid., 1:632.

11.   Ibid., 1:632, 638–39.

12.   Theodore Joslin, diary entry of Feb. 7, 1932, Box 1, Theodore Joslin Papers, Herbert C. Hoover Presidential Library, West Branch, Iowa (hereafter cited as HHPL).

13.   James H. MacLafferty, diary entry of Jan. 15, 1932, Box 2, James H. MacLafferty Papers, HIWRP.

14.   James H. MacLafferty, diary entry of Apr. 21, 1932, Box 2, MacLafferty Papers, HIWRP.

15.   Theodore Joslin, diary entry of Apr. 27, 1932, Box 1, Joslin Papers, HHPL.

16.   Theodore Joslin, diary entry of Apr. 30, 1932, Box 1, Joslin Papers, HHPL.

17.   Kenneth S. Davis, *FDR: The New York Years, 1928–1933* (New York: Random House, 1985), p. 300.

18.   Jim Farley, memorandum, Apr. 23, 1932, Box 82, Cuneo Papers, FRPL.

19.   "Roosevelt Hears of Whispering Plot," *New York Times,* May 16, 1932, p. 8.

20.   Elliott Roosevelt and James Brough, *An Untold Story: The Roosevelts of Hyde Park* (New York: G. P. Putnam's Sons, 1973), p. 303.

21.   Stephen Skowronek, "Franklin Roosevelt and the Modern Presidency," *Studies in American Political Development* 6 (1992): 327.

22.   "F. D. Roosevelt Will Fly Here to Accept Today," *Chicago Tribune,* July 2, 1932, p. 3.

23.   Arthur Sears Henning, "Nominee Flies to Convention; Speaks; Asks for a New Deal," *Chicago Tribune,* July 3, 1932, p. 1.

24.   Roy V. Peel and Thomas C. Donnelly, *The 1932 Campaign: An Analysis* (New York: Farrar & Rhinehart, 1935), pp. 103–104.

25.   Roosevelt and Brough, *An Untold Story,* p. 303.

26.   Lela Stiles, *The Man behind Roosevelt: The Story of Louis McHenry Howe* (Cleveland: World Publishing, 1954), p. 191.

27.   Quoted in Davis, *FDR: The New York Years,* p. 292.

28.   Davis, *FDR: The New York Years,* p. 292.

29.   "'The Country Needs, the Country Demands Bold, Persistent Experimentation,' Address at Oglethorpe University, May 22, 1932," in FDR, *The Public Papers and Addresses of Franklin D. Roosevelt,* 1:643.

30.   Ibid., 1:632.

31.   Theodore Joslin, diary entry of June 28, 1932, Box 1, Joslin Papers, HHPL.

32.   Theodore Joslin, diary entry of July 1, 1932, Box 1, Joslin Papers, HHPL.

33.   Franklin Roosevelt to the Chicago delegates, July 1, 1932. This handwritten note is framed and on display in the Roosevelt Museum at Hyde Park, N.Y.

34.   James H. MacLafferty, diary entry of July 2, 1932, Box 2, MacLafferty Papers, HIWRP.

35.   See Raymond Moley, *After Seven Years* (New York: Harper & Brothers, 1939), pp. 26–34.

36.   "'I Pledge You—I Pledge Myself to a New Deal for the American People': The Governor Accepts the Nomination for the Presidency, Chicago, Ill., July 2, 1932," in FDR, *The Public Papers and Addresses of Franklin D. Roosevelt,* 1:647.

37. Ibid., 1:648.

38. Ibid.

39. Ibid., 648, 649.

40. Ibid., 650.

41. Ibid.

42. Ibid., 1:651.

43. Ibid., 1:651, 657.

44. Ibid., 1:652.

45. Suzanne M. Daughton, "FDR as Family Doctor: Medical Metaphors and the Role of Physician in the Domestic Fireside Chats" (paper presented at the Speech Communication Association convention, New Orleans, La., November, 1994).

46. "'I Pledge You—I Pledge Myself to a New Deal,'" 1:658.

47. Ibid., 1:652.

48. Ibid., 1:654.

49. Ibid., 1:654, 655.

50. Richard Hofstadter, *The American Political Tradition and the Men Who Made It* (New York: Vintage, 1974), p. 398.

51. "'I Pledge You—I Pledge Myself to a New Deal,'" 1:656, 657.

52. Ibid., 1:658, 659.

53. "Mr. Roosevelt's Speech," *New York Times,* July 4, 1932, p. 10.

54. Claude G. Bowers, "The Battle Flag Unfurled," *New York Journal,* July 5, 1932, n.p.

Chapter 7

1. James H. MacLafferty, diary entry of July 22, 1932, Box 2, MacLafferty Papers, HIWRP.

2. "Article Number Two by Louis Howe," Dec. 15, 1932, Box 54, Howe Papers, FRPL.

3. Jim Farley, writings, memoranda, and related material, Box 82, Cuneo Papers, FRPL.

4. Ibid.; "Article Number Two by Louis Howe."

5. Raymond Moley, interview with Dr. Eliot A. Rosen, pp. 51–52, Series 1–3, Raymond Moley Oral History, HHPL.

6. Quoted in "Article Number Two by Louis Howe."

7. Quoted in "'Whispering Plot' Assailed by Farley," *New York Times,* July 31, 1932, p. 14.

8. "Topics of the Times," *New York Times,* Aug. 1, 1932, p. 14.

9. "Three Reasons Why Every Woman Should Vote for Roosevelt and Garner," flier in President's Subject File, Republican National Committee, Box 255, HHPL. The irony of this advertisement for the Roosevelt-Garner ticket is palpable: Roosevelt had not shared a bed with Eleanor since at least 1918, the date of her discovery of his affair with Lucy Mercer.

10. Speaker's Kit, Democratic National Campaign Committee Women's Division, President's Subject File, Republican National Committee, Box 255, HHPL.

11. "Half a Million Life Insurance," DNCC flier, Box 15, Lewis L. Strauss Papers, HHPL.

12. "Campaign Book of the Democratic Party Candidates and Issues 1932," President's Subject File, Republican National Committee, Box 253, HHPL.

13. "Franklin D. Roosevelt: Who He Is, What He Has Done," President's Subject File, Republican National Committee, Box 254, HHPL.

14. FDR, Informal Extemporaneous Remarks of Governor Roosevelt, Goodland, Kansas, Sept. 15, 1932, FDR Speech File, File 500, Box 10, FDR Papers, FRPL.

15. *Brooklyn Daily Eagle,* n.d., clipping in Campaign Scrapbook, Sept.12–Oct. 7, 1932, FDR Papers, FRPL.

16. "The Economics of Original Sin," *The Business Week,* Apr. 23, 1930, p. 48.

17. "The Castor-Oil School of Economics," *The Business Week,* July 9, 1930, p. 40.

18. Elaine Scarry, *The Body in Pain: The Making and Unmaking of the World* (New York: Oxford University Press, 1985), p. 14.

19. F. W. Taussig, "Doctors, Economists, and the Depression," *Harper's,* August, 1932, p. 359.

20. "Major Surgery for the Depression," *New Republic,* Nov. 2, 1932, p. 315.

21. Roger W. Babson, "Everybody Has a Job," *World's Work,* February, 1931, p. 67.

22. Roger W. Babson, "How to Cure the Blues," *Collier's,* Mar. 28, 1931, p. 62.

23. James Bayard Clark, "A Doctor Looks at Economics," *Review of Reviews,* June, 1932, p. 29.

24. Louis T. McFadden, "Convalescent Finance," *Saturday Evening Post,* Feb. 15, 1930, p. 5.

25. Walter Lippmann, "A Reckoning: Twelve Years of Republican Rule," *Yale Review,* June, 1932, p. 657.

26. "Nature's Course," *Saturday Evening Post,* Oct. 1, 1932, p. 20.

27. "In the Soothsayer's Season," *The Business Week,* Dec. 25, 1929, p. 36.

28. William Trufant Foster, "When a Horse Balks," *North American Review,* July, 1932, p. 4.

29. Nelson H. Cruikshank, "Prosperity by Suggestion," *World Tomorrow,* March, 1931, p. 85.

30. For studies detailing Hoover's confidence-based approach to economics, see Davis W. Houck, *Rhetoric as Currency: Hoover, Roosevelt and the Great Depression* (College Station: Texas A&M University Press, 2001); William J. Barber, *From New Era to New Deal* (Cambridge: Cambridge University Press, 1985); Albert U. Romasco, *The Poverty of Abundance: Hoover, the Nation, the Depression* (New York: Oxford University Press, 1965); Jordan Schwarz, *The Interregnum of Despair: Hoover, Congress, and the Depression* (Urbana: University of Illinois Press, 1970); Stephen Skowronek, *The Politics Presidents Make: Leadership from John Adams to George Bush* (Cambridge, Mass.: Belknap Press of Harvard University Press, 1993); Theodore G. Joslin, *Hoover Off the Record* (Garden City, N.Y.: Doubleday, Doran, 1934).

31. Edwin F. Gay, "The Great Depression," *Foreign Affairs,* July, 1932, p. 529.

32. "One Hundred Doses, One Dollar," *Saturday Evening Post,* September 26, 1931, p. 22.

33. "The Failures of the Preceding Administration: Campaign Address at Columbus, Ohio, August 20, 1932," in FDR, *The Public Papers and Addresses of Franklin D. Roosevelt,* 1:683.

34. "'A Restored and Rehabilitated Agriculture': Campaign Address on the Farm Problem at Topeka, Kans., September 14, 1932," in FDR, *The Public Papers and Addresses of Franklin D. Roosevelt,* 1:698.

35. Ibid., 1:705.

36. "'The Railroad Mesh Is the Warp on Which Our Economic Web Is Largely Fashioned': Campaign Address on Railroads at Salt Lake City, Utah, September 17, 1932," in FDR, *The Public Papers and Addresses of Franklin D. Roosevelt,* 1:721–22.

37. Ibid., 1:712.

38. "Campaign Address on Reciprocal Tariff Negotiations, Seattle, Wash., September 20, 1932," in FDR, *The Public Papers and Addresses of Franklin D. Roosevelt,* 1:725.

39. "Roosevelt Pays Visit to Crippled Children," *Seattle Times,* Sept. 21, 1932, clipping in Campaign Scrapbook, Sept. 12–Oct. 7, 1932, FDR Papers, FRPL.

40. "Campaign Address on Agriculture and Tariffs, Sioux City, Iowa, September 29, 1932," in FDR, *The Public Papers and Addresses of Franklin D. Roosevelt,* 1:767–68.

41. Informal Remarks at the Hollywood Bowl, Sept. 24, 1932, FDR Speech Files, File 526, Box 12, FDR Papers, FRPL.

42. "Address of Governor Franklin D. Roosevelt, Naval Armory, Belle Isle Bridge, Detroit, Michigan, October 2, 1932," FDR Speech Files, File 548, Box 12, FDR Papers, FRPL.

43. Ibid.

44. Quoted in "Roosevelt Is Fit, Copeland Asserts," *New York Times,* Sept. 15, 1932, p. 16.

45. Quoted in "Pioneer Goes West," *Time,* Sept. 26, 1932, p. 10.

46. Quoted in "Slurs on Roosevelt Charged by Garvan," *New York Times,* Sept. 19, 1932, p. 9.

47. Josephus Daniels, "Franklin Roosevelt As I Know Him," *Saturday Evening Post,* Sept. 24, 1932, p. 80.

48. Colonel House [Edward Mandell House], interviewed by Tyler Mason, n.d., p. 1, Roosevelt Family Papers Donated by Children, Political Files 1929–33, Box 23, FDR Papers, FRPL.

49. Dr. Edgar W. Beckwith to Franklin D. Roosevelt, Oct. 21, 1932, Box 54, Howe Papers, FRPL.

50. A. H. Levens to Adolf A. Berle, Sept. 24, 1932, Box 15, Adolf A. Berle Papers, FRPL.

51. M. L. Wilson to Raymond Moley, Sept. 21, 1932, "Campaign of 1932," Moley Papers, HIWRP.

52. "Article Number Two by Louis Howe."

53. "Campaign Address on the Federal Budget at Pittsburgh, Pa., October 19, 1932," in FDR, *The Public Papers and Addresses of Franklin D. Roosevelt,* 1:803.

54. Ibid., 1:807, 811.

55. "'I Am Waging a War in This Campaign against the Four Horsemen of the Present Republican Leadership: Destruction, Delay, Deceit, Despair,' Campaign Address at Baltimore, Md., October 25, 1932," in FDR, *The Public Papers and Address of Franklin D. Roosevelt,* 1:832.

56. Ibid., 1:840.

57. Robert Barry, "9,000 Miles with Franklin D. Roosevelt," *The Democratic Bulletin,* November, 1932, p. 10.

58. *The Times* (London), Nov. 5, 1932, p. 10d.

59. FDR, "Radio Broadcast, Sunday Night, October 30, 1932, at 10:56 P.M. Subject: Welfare & Relief Mobilization of 1932," FDR Speech Files, File 559, Box 12, FDR Papers, FRPL.

60. FDR, "Governor Roosevelt's Address," Brooklyn Academy of Music, Friday, Nov. 4, 1932, FDR Speech Files, File 584, Box 12, FDR Papers, FRPL.

61. "'I Believe That the Best Interests of the Country Require a Change in Administration': Campaign Address at Madison Square Garden, New York City, November 5, 1932," in FDR, *The Public Papers and Addresses of Franklin D. Roosevelt,* 1:862–63.

62. Ibid., 1:863.

63. FDR, "Address of Governor Roosevelt," Nov. 7, 1932, FDR Speech Files, File 593, Box 12, FDR Papers, FRPL.

64. Quoted in Freidel, *Franklin D. Roosevelt: The Triumph,* p. 371.

65. Quoted in James Roosevelt and Sidney Shalett, *Affectionately, F. D. R.: A Son's Story of a Lonely Man* (New York: Harcourt, Brace, 1959), p. 232.

Chapter 8

1. See Richard M. Weaver, "The Spaciousness of Old Rhetoric," in Weaver, *The Ethics of Rhetoric* (Chicago: Henry Regnery, 1953; reprint, Davis, Calif.: Hermagoras Press, 1983).

2. Quoted in Geoffrey C. Ward, ed., *Closest Companion: The Unknown Story of the Intimate Friendship between Franklin Roosevelt and Margaret Suckley* (Boston: Houghton Mifflin, 1995), p. 5.

3. "Campaign Address at Chicago, Ill.: 'It Was This Administration Which Saved the System of Private Profit and Free Enterprise,' October 14, 1936," in FDR, *The Public Papers and Addresses of Franklin D. Roosevelt,* 5:488.

4. Garry Wills, *Certain Trumpets: The Call of Leaders* (New York: Simon & Schuster, 1994), p. 32.

BIBLIOGRAPHY

Archival Collections

Berle, Adolf A., Jr. Papers. Franklin D. Roosevelt Presidential Library, Hyde Park, N.Y.

Cuneo, Ernest. Papers. Franklin D. Roosevelt Presidential Library, Hyde Park, N.Y.

Halsted, Anna Roosevelt. Papers. Franklin D. Roosevelt Presidential Library, Hyde Park, N.Y.

Hoover, Herbert C. Papers. Herbert C. Hoover Presidential Library, West Branch, Iowa.

Howe, Louis McHenry. Papers. Franklin D. Roosevelt Presidential Library, Hyde Park, N.Y.

Joslin, Theodore. Papers. Herbert C. Hoover Presidential Library, West Branch, Iowa.

MacLafferty, James H. Papers. Hoover Institution on War, Revolution and Peace, Stanford, Calif.

Moley, Raymond. Oral History. Herbert C. Hoover Presidential Library, West Branch, Iowa.

———. Papers. Hoover Institution on War, Revolution and Peace, Stanford, Calif.

Roosevelt, Eleanor. Papers. Franklin D. Roosevelt Presidential Library, Hyde Park, N.Y.

Roosevelt, Franklin D. Papers. Franklin D. Roosevelt Presidential Library, Hyde Park, N.Y.

Strauss, Lewis L. Papers. Herbert C. Hoover Presidential Library, West Branch, Iowa.

Books and Articles

Arnold, Carroll C. "Oral Rhetoric, Rhetoric, and Literature." *Philosophy & Rhetoric* 1 (1968): 191–210.

Babson, Roger W. "Everybody Has a Job." *World's Work,* February, 1931, pp. 67–69.

———. "How to Cure the Blues." *Collier's,* March 28, 1931, pp. 12–13, 60–63.

Barber, William J. *From New Era to New Deal.* Cambridge: Cambridge University Press, 1985.

Barry, Robert. "9,000 Miles with Franklin D. Roosevelt." *The Democratic Bulletin,* November, 1932, pp. 10, 45.

"Big Welcome Planned for Roosevelt." *Syracuse Journal,* October 23, 1928, p. 2.

Bitzer, Lloyd F. "The Rhetorical Situation." *Philosophy & Rhetoric* 1 (1968): 1–14.

Blair, Carole. "Contemporary U.S. Memorial Sites as Exemplars of Rhetorical Materiality." Pp. 16–57 in *Rhetorical Bodies,* edited by Jack Selzer and Sharon Crowley. Madison: University of Wisconsin Press, 1999.

Bowers, Claude G. "The Battle Flag Unfurled." *New York Journal,* July 5, 1932, n.p.

Brueggemann, Brenda Jo, and James A. Fredal. "Studying Disability Rhetorically." Pp. 129–35 in *Disability Discourse,* edited by Mairian Corker and Sally French. Buckingham, England: Open University Press, 1999.

Burke, Kenneth. *Language as Symbolic Action.* Berkeley: University of California Press, 1968.

Campbell, Karlyn Kohrs, and Kathleen Hall Jamieson. *Deeds Done in Words: Presidential Rhetoric and the Genres of Governance.* Chicago: University of Chicago Press, 1990.

"The Castor-Oil School of Economics." *The Business Week,* July 9, 1930, p. 40.

Clark, James Bayard. "A Doctor Looks at Economics." *Review of Reviews,* June, 1932, pp. 29–31.

Connell, R. W. *Masculinities.* Berkeley: University of California Press, 1995.

Corker, Mairian, and Sally French. "Reclaiming Discourse in Disability Studies." Pp. 1–11 in *Disability Discourse,* edited by Mairian Corker and Sally French. Buckingham, England: Open University Press, 1999.

Crispell, Kenneth R., and Carlos F. Gomez. *Hidden Illness in the White House.* Durham, N.C.: Duke University Press, 1988.

Cruikshank, Nelson H. "Prosperity by Suggestion." *World Tomorrow,* March, 1931, pp. 85–87.

Daniels, Josephus. "Franklin Roosevelt As I Know Him." *Saturday Evening Post,* September 24, 1932, p. 80.

Daughton, Suzanne M. "FDR as Family Doctor: Medical Metaphors and the Role of Physician in the Domestic Fireside Chats." Paper presented at Speech Communication Association meeting, New Orleans, La., November, 1994.

Davis, Kenneth S. *FDR: The New York Years, 1928–1933.* New York: Random House, 1985.

———. *Invincible Summer: An Intimate Portrait of the Roosevelts Based on the Recollections of Marion Dickerman.* New York: Atheneum, 1974.

Davis, Lennard J. Introduction to *The Disability Studies Reader,* edited by
    Lennard J. Davis. New York: Routledge, 1997.

"The Economics of Original Sin." *The Business Week,* April 23, 1930, p. 48.

Edwards, George C., III. "Presidential Rhetoric: What Difference Does It
    Make?" Pp. 199–217 in *Beyond the Rhetorical Presidency,* edited by
    Martin J. Medhurst. College Station: Texas A&M University Press,
    1996.

"F. D. Roosevelt Ill of Poliomyelitis." *New York Times,* September 16, 1921,
    p. 1.

"F. D. Roosevelt Will Fly Here to Accept Today." *Chicago Tribune,* July 2, 1932,
    p. 3.

"Fine Character of Roosevelt Wins Support." *Times of Batavia (New York),*
    October 20, 1928, p. 1.

"A Flattering Campaign." *New York Times,* October 17, 1928, p. 28.

Foster, William Trufant. "When a Horse Balks." *North American Review,*
    July, 1932, pp. 4–10.

Foucault, Michel. *The Archaeology of Knowledge and the Discourse on
    Language.* Translated by A. M. Sheridan Smith. New York: Pantheon,
    1972.

"Franklin D. Roosevelt Better." *New York Times,* August 29, 1921, p. 11.

"Franklin D. Roosevelt Democratic Choice." *Times of Batavia (New York),*
    November 3, 1928, p. 6.

"Franklin D. Roosevelt Ill." *New York Times,* August 27, 1921, p. 9.

"Franklin D. Roosevelt Improving." *New York Times,* September 10, 1921,
    p. 4.

"Franklin Roosevelt Speaks Here." *Daily Messenger (Canandaigua, N.Y.),*
    October 23, 1928, p. 1.

Freidel, Frank. *Franklin D. Roosevelt: The Ordeal.* Boston: Little, Brown, 1954.

———. *Franklin D. Roosevelt: The Triumph.* Boston: Little, Brown, 1956.

Gallagher, Hugh Gregory. *FDR's Splendid Deception.* New York: Dodd, Mead,
    1985.

Gay, Edwin F. "The Great Depression." *Foreign Affairs,* July, 1932, pp. 529–40.

Goldberg, Richard Thayer. *The Making of Franklin D. Roosevelt: Triumph over
    Disability.* Cambridge, Mass.: Abt, 1981.

Gould, Jean. *A Good Fight: The Story of F.D.R.'s Conquest of Polio.* New York:
    Dodd, Mead, 1960.

Gunther, John. *Roosevelt in Retrospect: A Profile in History.* New York: Harper,
    1950.

Hart, Roderick P. *The Sound of Leadership: Presidential Communication in the
    Modern Age.* Chicago: University of Chicago Press, 1987.

"Health Forbids Acceptance, Is Roosevelt Wire." *Elmira (New York) Advertiser,*
    October 2, 1928, p. 1.

Henning, Arthur Sears. "Nominee Flies to Convention; Speaks; Asks for a
    New Deal." *Chicago Tribune,* July 3, 1932, p. 1.

Hirsch, Karen. "Culture and Disability: The Role of Oral History." *Oral History Review* 22 (1995): 1–27.

Hofstadter, Richard. *The American Political Tradition and the Men Who Made It.* New York: Vintage, 1974.

Homer. *The Iliad.* Translated by Robert Fagles. New York: Viking, 1997.

Houck, Davis W. *Rhetoric as Currency: Hoover, Roosevelt, and the Great Depression.* College Station: Texas A&M University Press, 2001.

"In the Soothsayer's Season." *The Business Week,* December 25, 1929, p. 36.

Joslin, Theodore G. *Hoover Off the Record.* Garden City, N.Y.: Doubleday, Doran, 1934.

Kimmel, Michael S. "Consuming Manhood: The Feminization of American Culture and the Recreation of the Male Body, 1832–1920." *Michigan Quarterly Review* 33 (1994): 7–33.

———. "Invisible Masculinity." *Society* 30 (1993): 28–35.

Klages, Mary. *Woeful Afflictions: Disability and Sentimentality in Victorian America.* Philadelphia: University of Pennsylvania Press, 1999.

Lee, Robert M. "Nothing But Smith as Gentlemen from Bowery Pack Gallery." *Los Angeles Times,* June 27, 1924, p. 3.

Linton, Simi. *Claiming Disability: Knowledge and Identity.* New York: New York University Press, 1998.

Lippman, Theo, Jr. *The Squire of Warm Springs: F.D.R. in Georgia, 1924–1945.* Chicago: Playboy Press, 1977.

Lippmann, Walter. "A Reckoning: Twelve Years of Republican Rule." *Yale Review,* June, 1932, pp. 649–60.

Looker, Earle. "Is Franklin D. Roosevelt Physically Fit to Be President?" *Liberty Magazine,* July 25, 1931, pp. 6–10.

———. *This Man Roosevelt.* New York: Brewer, Warren & Putnam, 1932.

"Major Surgery for the Depression." *New Republic,* November 2, 1932, pp. 314–15.

McFadden, Louis T. "Convalescent Finance." *Saturday Evening Post,* February 15, 1930, p. 5.

Meekosha, Helen. "Body Battles: Bodies, Gender and Disability." Pp. 163–80 in *The Disability Reader: Social Science Perspectives,* edited by Tom Shakespeare. London: Cassell, 1998.

Mitchell, David T., and Sharon L. Snyder. "Introduction: Disability Studies and the Double Bind of Representation." Pp. 1–31 in *The Body and Physical Difference: Discourses of Disability,* edited by David T. Mitchell and Sharon L. Snyder. Ann Arbor: University of Michigan Press, 1998.

Moley, Raymond. *After Seven Years.* New York: Harper & Brothers, 1939.

"Mr. Roosevelt's Speech." *New York Times,* July 4, 1932, p. 10.

"Nature's Course." *Saturday Evening Post,* October 1, 1932, p. 20.

"Nominee of Party Stops at Herkimer." *Utica (New York) Observer-Dispatch,* October 26, 1928, p. 1.

Norton, Anne. *Republic of Signs: Liberal Theory and American Popular Culture.* Chicago: University of Chicago Press, 1993.

"One Hundred Doses, One Dollar." *Saturday Evening Post,* September 26, 1931, p. 22.

Oulahan, Richard V. "Governor Smith Is Put in Nomination Amid Wild Cheers." *New York Times,* June 28, 1928, p. 1.

Outram, Dorinda. *The Body and the French Revolution: Sex, Class, and Political Culture.* New Haven: Yale University Press, 1989.

Palmer, Kyle D. "Ku Klux Hood and Gown Foil Democratic Craft." *Los Angeles Times,* June 27, 1924, p. 6.

Peel, Roy V., and Thomas C. Donnelly. *The 1932 Campaign: An Analysis.* New York: Farrar & Rhinehart, 1935.

Perkins, Frances. *The Roosevelt I Knew.* New York: Viking, 1946.

"Pioneer Goes West." *Time,* September 26, 1932, p. 10.

"Political Notes." *Time,* June 15, 1931, p. 17.

"Prohibition." *Time,* April 27, 1931, p. 18.

Rogers, Naomi. *Dirt and Disease: Polio before FDR.* New Brunswick, N.J.: Rutgers University Press, 1992.

Rollins, Alfred B. *Roosevelt and Howe.* New York: Knopf, 1962.

Romasco, Albert U. *The Poverty of Abundance: Hoover, the Nation, the Depression.* New York: Oxford University Press, 1965.

Roosevelt, Elliott, ed. *F.D.R.: His Personal Letters.* Vol. 2, *1905–1928.* New York: Duell, Sloan and Pearce, 1950.

Roosevelt, Elliott, and James Brough. *An Untold Story: The Roosevelts of Hyde Park.* New York: G. P. Putnam's Sons, 1973.

Roosevelt, Franklin D. *The Public Papers and Addresses of Franklin D. Roosevelt.* Vols. 1 and 2. Compiled by Samuel I. Rosenman. New York: Random House, 1938.

"Roosevelt Accepts Nomination." *Elmira (New York) Advertiser,* October 3, 1928, p. 1.

"Roosevelt Hears of Whispering Plot." *New York Times,* May 16, 1932, p. 8.

"Roosevelt Is Fit, Copeland Asserts." *New York Times,* September 15, 1932, p. 16.

Roosevelt, James, and Sidney Shalett. *Affectionately, F. D. R.: A Son's Story of a Lonely Man.* New York: Harcourt, Brace, 1959.

Rotundo, E. Anthony. "Body and Soul: Changing Ideals of American Middle-Class Manhood, 1770–1920." *Journal of Social History* 16 (1983): 23–38.

"Rum Not State Issue, Says Roosevelt." *Syracuse Journal,* October 24, 1928, p. 2.

Scarry, Elaine. *The Body in Pain: The Making and Unmaking of the World.* New York: Oxford University Press, 1985.

Schwarz, Jordan. *The Interregnum of Despair: Hoover, Congress, and the Depression.* Urbana: University of Illinois Press, 1970.

Selzer, Jack. "Habeas Corpus: An Introduction." Pp. 3–15 in *Rhetorical Bodies,* edited by Jack Selzer and Sharon Crowley. Madison: University of Wisconsin Press, 1999.

Skowronek, Stephen. "Franklin Roosevelt and the Modern Presidency." *Studies in American Political Development* 6 (1992): 322–58.

———. *The Politics Presidents Make: Leadership from John Adams to George Bush.* Cambridge, Mass.: Belknap Press of Harvard University Press, 1993.

"Slurs on Roosevelt Charged by Garvan." *New York Times,* September 19, 1932, p. 9.

Stiles, Lela. *The Man behind Roosevelt: The Story of Louis McHenry Howe.* Cleveland: World Publishing, 1954.

Taussig, F. W. "Doctors, Economists, and the Depression." *Harper's,* August, 1932, pp. 355–65.

"Topics of the Times." *New York Times,* August 1, 1932, p. 14.

Tugwell, Rexford G. *The Brains Trust.* New York: Viking, 1968.

"An Unfair Sacrifice." *New York Herald Tribune,* October 3, 1928, p. 26.

Ward, Geoffrey C. *A First-Class Temperament: The Emergence of Franklin Roosevelt.* New York: Harper & Row, 1989.

———, ed. *Closest Companion: The Unknown Story of the Intimate Friendship between Franklin Roosevelt and Margaret Suckley.* Boston: Houghton Mifflin, 1995.

Weaver, Richard M. *The Ethics of Rhetoric.* Chicago: Henry Regnery, 1953; reprint, Davis, Calif.: Hermagoras Press, 1983.

"'Whispering Plot' Assailed by Farley." *New York Times,* July 31, 1932, p. 14.

Wills, Garry. *Certain Trumpets: The Call of Leaders.* New York: Simon & Schuster, 1994.

Wilson, James C., and Cynthia Lewiecki-Wilson. "Disability, Rhetoric, and the Body." Pp. 1–24 in *Embodied Rhetorics: Disability in Language and Culture,* edited by James C. Wilson and Cynthia Lewiecki-Wilson. Carbondale: Southern Illinois University Press, 2001.

Index